D0982668

THE NEW EXPLORATION

a philosophy of regional planning

UNIVERSITY OF ILLINOIS PRESS, URBANA, 1962

THE NEW EXPLORATION

by Benton MacKaye

with an introduction by Lewis Mumford

Third printing of the paperback edition, 1972

Copyright 1928 by Harcourt, Brace and Company, Inc. Copyright 1956 by Benton MacKaye. © 1962 by the Board of Trustees of the University of Illinois. Manufactured in the United States of America. Library of Congress Catalog Card No. 62-17516.

ISBN 0-252-72581-6

To
SHIRLEY CENTER
An Indigenous Community

INTRODUCTION

The New Exploration is a book that deserves a place on the same shelf that holds Henry Thoreau's *Walden* and George Perkins Marsh's *Man and Nature;* and like the first of these books, it has had to wait a whole generation to acquire the readers that would appreciate it. In the field of regional planning Benton MacKaye's book was not merely a pioneer essay in its own time, but it is still ahead of much of the thinking and planning being done in this field today, since too little of that effort displays either the hard logic or the humane insight MacKaye has brought to the subject.

In Benton MacKaye the voice of an older America, a voice with echoes not only of Thoreau, but of Davy Crockett, Audubon, and Mark Twain, addresses itself to the problem of how to use the natural and cultural resources we have at hand today without defacing the landscape, polluting the atmosphere, disrupting the complex associations of animal and plant species upon which all higher life depends, and thus in the end destroying the possibilities for further human development. That voice was needed in 1928; and because it was not listened to, it is needed even more today.

In the course of this last generation, MacKaye's timely diagnosis has proved sound; and his well-grounded forebodings have been confirmed even more rapidly than he anticipated. Nobody else in our time has pointed out more clearly the terms upon which modern man, and in particular the American people, may occupy the earth and use judiciously all our resources, natural, technical, and urban, without making the land itself uninhabitable and our own life unendurable. If this book seems at times as elementary as an old-fashioned spelling book, that very quality carries a recognition of the fact that in dealing with the earth itself and man's habitations and fabrications, we have still to learn our ABC's.

Perhaps the best way to appreciate the special nature of *The New Exploration* is to take a look at the life of the man who wrote it. Benton MacKaye, as his last name indicates, is a member of a great clan, not the least of whom was his father, the actor and playwright, Steele MacKaye. Steele MacKaye was a man of such intrepid nature that he could, the legend goes, calm down a lion by looking him in the eye: it is at least on record that on a visit to the zoo his hand was somehow grabbed by an arctic fox; but instead of pulling away, Steele pushed his hand farther into the animal's mouth, not merely making the fox let go but completing his conquest by stroking him. All the MacKaye boys had character: human lions and foxes never daunted them.

Born in Stamford, Connecticut, in 1879, MacKaye spent the early years of his life, like his fellow Yankee, Robert Frost, outside his native region; for until he was nine he lived in Manhattan. So, though MacKaye is pre-eminently a man of the outdoors — a founder and a past president of the Wilderness Society — he retains, beneath the butternut-dyed, homespun togs of the old-fashioned Yankee, the sophistication of the aboriginal New Yorker, and a Harvard graduate to boot. No one could have written such a clear appreciation of the respective virtues of the primeval, the rural, and the urban environments as MacKaye has done, if he were not equally familiar with all three of them.

But young Benton was fortunate in that his family migrated to an old, almost untouched New England village, Shirley Center, when he was nine. This village lies in the midst of gentle open country like that which surrounds Concord: an environment whose very tameness challenged both Thoreau and MacKaye to seek and sample every patch of virgin nature they could find; and as late as the end of the nineteenth century many active survivals of the old rural culture were still visible and audible. Even today, despite the very ominous encroachments of the Boston conurbation, there are still plenty of frogs in the woodlands and marshes to greet in chorus the spring; so that one of the most moving passages MacKaye ever wrote was prompted recently by hearing those sounds and reflecting that the voice of the frogs was probably the first sound that broke the silence of creation in the carboniferous period, and so modern coal-using man is joined to those ancient days, by sound as well as by the heat of his steel furnaces.

In New York, young MacKaye had only been a visitor, or worse, a prisoner, chafing to escape. As soon as he reached Shirley, he knew he was home; and from that time on this village has been the center of his life, despite many prolonged absences: it served from the beginning as the base line for many of his activities, combining as it did the sturdy self-sustaining social life of the New England town or village, with its school, its church, its town hall, the essential local organs of all culture worthy of the name, based on farms that were for long in active operation, with a somewhat wilder background, full of botanical and animal life, which beckoned him. If the reader chances to recall the New England village as presented in the old documentary film, *The City* (1939), he will have retained glimpses of MacKaye's favorite habitat.

From this center, before he reached adolescence, young Benton went on divers rambles with his brother James and other village boys, exploring the miniature valley of Mulpus Brook or the "wilds" of the Squanacook River. "These walks," he reports, "were just walks; I revelled in them, but I did not *do* anything with them. And this worried me." In the spring of 1893, at the age of fourteen, he became inspired to *do* something with his walks: he sought to imitate Humboldt and describe the far lands within his walking radius; more particularly, he decided to map the forest areas, dividing them between "evergreen" and "deciduous." In his characteristic systematic way, MacKaye laid out a whole series of walks and dignified them, again with thoughts of Humboldt, by calling them "expeditions." On one of these expeditions, he not merely accompanied his United States topographic map with a brief narrative, but tore loose with philosophic reflections in a language all his own. This happened to be his ninth expedition; and from that time on his brother James, who discovered Benton's opus and liked to recite high-flown passages from it with great glee, used to call this broader kind of nature study "expedition nining."

In a very real sense MacKaye's whole life has been one long Expedition Nine: the work of a mind that reveled in nature, but was worried about mere private enjoyment of the wilderness until he did something about it: studying its primeval order and its human uses, and translating both his enjoyment and his practical insight into such a form as to preserve for the rest of the community the values that he had found for himself. Spontaneously, as a boy, MacKaye had worked out for himself the method of regional survey which, unbeknown to him, Patrick Geddes and his colleagues were already developing at the Outlook Tower in Edinburgh. When the two men met at the Hudson Guild Farm in 1923, they understood each other at once; and in front of the portrait of Humboldt at the American Museum of Natural History, a little later, they told each other of the influence that this great mind had had on them.

Expedition Nine shows that MacKaye was from the beginning a regional planner by intention as well as by instinct. Remarkably enough, young Charles Eliot II and his brother, only a little while before, had been wandering over the less settled parts of Greater Boston on weekends, spotting the more beautiful stretches of landscape that might be preserved for the future by being turned into parks. Those youthful sorties gave Charles Eliot his start as a landscape architect; and made it possible for him to plan, in an astonishingly short period, the magnificent series of parks he laid out for the Boston Metropolitan Parks System. I point out the parallel between these two New England planners to emphasize the importance of autonomous education, through solitary rambles and explorations, which we are now losing by an almost totalitarian emphasis upon group activities cut to a standard pattern; likewise, the importance of dreaming audaciously when one is young. Though one can assign a rough date to the moment when MacKaye consciously decided to become a forester (1903) or propose the Appalachian Trail (1921) I should guess that a glimmer of both ideas came to him first on these boyhood walks. There is a place for crowds and shared activities; but there should also be a place for the lonely soul to commune with himself and dream freely, dream boldly. In his advocacy of public protection for wilderness areas MacKaye never forgot that lesson of his own life.

This direct, first-hand education through the senses and feelings, with its deliberate observation of nature in every guise — including the human animal — has nourished MacKaye all his life; and it is no doubt partly responsible for his fresh way of attacking many problems that his colleagues have too often approached, if at all, by way of information derived from books, which have themselves often been composed of other books. If the sea was Herman Melville's Yale College and Harvard, the natural landscape served as the same school for MacKaye, whether he approached it as a boy explorer, as a forester, as a conservationist, or as a regional planner for the Tennessee Valley Authority (1934-1936) and the Rural Electrification Administration (1942-1945). But MacKaye was fortunate in having that education rounded out at Harvard in its halcyon period at the beginning of the present century; for he sat at the feet of two redoubtable geographic scholars, Nathaniel Southgate Shaler and William Morris Davis. Davis's analysis of the landscape in terms of structure, process, and stage, was in its way as clarifying as Patrick Geddes's approach to society by way of folk, work, and place.

Though MacKaye got his M.A. in forestry in 1905, and taught forestry at Harvard for a few years, his main activities, from 1905 to 1918, centered in the United States Forest Service, both in Washington and in the field. This was one of the culminating points of the conservation movement, whose foundations had first been laid by the classic study of man's relation to the earth, by George Perkins Marsh, a survey in which Marsh had demonstrated that one civilization after another had been undermined by the removal of the forest cover, with not only an exhaustion of the wood supply, but the erosion of soils, the flooding of valleys, and even, in all probability, the changing of climatic conditions. Under the inspiration of W J McGee, who drafted the basic reports of the Conservation Commission, the conservation movement which aimed at replenishing the wasted resources had gotten under way, zealously and strenuously backed by President Theodore Roosevelt.

Roosevelt had supported the public-spirited Gifford Pinchot as head of the Forestry Bureau; and Benton MacKaye was one of Pinchot's young men, primarily engaged in reclaiming and improving the forests of America; but also concerned, like his superior, with the wider issues of conservation as applied to all the basic natural resources — soils and minerals as well as trees. MacKaye helped to draft a bill introduced in the Congress to conserve, through public ownership and control, the essential resources of the last American frontier, that of Alaska; and this same concern for conserving human values as well as material ones caused him to spend a year (1918-1919) as a specialist in colonization, in the United States Department of Labor, working under that admirable Single Taxer, Louis Post, on a scheme, all too soon abandoned, to settle groups of returning soldiers on the land.

During this period in Washington MacKaye was one of a company of remarkable men, young and not so young, whose ideas and activities contributed to that great ferment in social thought, that quickening of the "social conscience," as it was then called, which fomented the Progressive movement among the Republicans and brought Woodrow Wilson into the White House. MacKaye's particular group of government workers and newspapermen included people as diverse as Stuart Chase, Judson King, and William L. Stoddard, the Washington correspondent of the then important *Boston Transcript*. They met once a fortnight for discussion: some interested in lessening economic waste, others in promoting good forest management, others in conserving water power for the whole community, rather than profits for electric power and light companies, others in adding to the wild recreation areas and restoring wildlife threatened with extinction: all of them devoted to improving the health, welfare, and happiness of their fellow countrymen, and in preserving for future generations basic resources that originally had belonged to the nation, and should never have been turned over so unreservedly to short-sighted, voracious, and irresponsible private owners.

These men were carrying on the work begun long before by Thoreau, when he advocated setting aside forests, in each community, for public use; for Thoreau had realized that the primeval background was an essential birthright that Americans, even in his time, were all too eagerly surrendering for a mess of pottage. His ideas were translated into action after the Civil War by Frederick Law Olmsted, who first proposed and helped secure the setting aside of national parks and national forests; and they were carried into other territory by John Wesley Powell, who pointed to the national importance of keeping intact for grazing the buffalo grass cover of the drier prairies instead of letting the soil be broken by the plow, to become the dust bowl that a heedless system of land settlement later allowed it to become.

Some day the history of this group will, one hopes, be written, along with that of another small group that MacKaye joined in New York in 1923, the Regional Planning Association of America. These keen, earnest, socially responsible minds influenced each other and fortified each other; and even as they had built on the work of the earlier conservationists, so in turn they laid the foundations for many of the important measures of the Roosevelt administration during the thirties: the TVA, rural electrification, rural resettlement, flood control, the shelter belt, reforestation by the conservation corps, and the series of regional planning studies undertaken by the National Resources Planning Board.

The high energies of this period were momentarily raised to a peak by America's contribution to the first World War, under Woodrow Wilson's farsighted and masterly leadership. The sudden spiritual deflation that followed in 1919, underlined by the physical paralysis of Wilson himself, was accompanied by the financial inflation and ostentatious material prosperity of the next decade. That was the decade of "normalcy," dominated by the financial wizards whose unscrupulous and reckless conduct brought on the economic depression of the thirties; and it was undermined increasingly by malevolent gangsters who battened on this general demoralization: a time when respectable citizens connived with bootleggers to break the law and defy the Constitution, only to find that criminal racketeers, specialists in torture and murder, were also muscling into trades unions and levying taxes upon respectable commercial enterprises, bribing judges, intimidating juries, creating huge feudal strongholds of corruption that are still far from being liquidated. But under the surface, deeper currents, whose source was in the same America that had nourished MacKaye, were still flowing; and not the least evidence of that life and that energy was the work that MacKaye undertook during this same decade.

At a moment when most Americans were flamboyantly preoccupied with liquor and sex, with rising stocks and multiplying motor cars, concerned only with the ephemeral things that money will buy, MacKaye went into retreat. Since, to pursue his ideas, he had abandoned government service, that retreat was almost a monastic one, comparable to Thoreau's at Walden: he wasted almost no time on earning a living, but, by tightening his belt and accepting what the ravens brought him, he concentrated on the main business of life, namely living; and this, in middle life, was for him more and more centered on fresh ideas for improving the habitability of the country he dearly loved.

The first manifestation of this new phase in his career was the article he contributed to the *Journal of the American Institute of Architects,* in October 1921, in which he outlined the project for an Appalachian footpath from Maine to Georgia. This was a remarkable subject to come forth in a professional architectural journal; and its appearance in those pages was due to the friendly encouragement and bold editorial policy of Charles Harris Whitaker, its editor. It was not merely in proposing a trail of such length that MacKaye's article made such a decisive departure: he conceived this new trail as the backbone of a whole system of wild reservations and parks, linking together by feeder trails into a grand system, to constitute a reservoir for maintaining the primeval and the rural environment at their highest levels. In the development of this Appalachian hinterland, MacKaye saw a means of designing a better urban pattern for the flow of population that was already making the whole coastal area from Boston to Washington into a formless "conurbation," as Patrick Geddes had long ago called it, before Jean Gottmann, in a recent study, gave it the less accurate name of "megalopolis."

I well remember the shock of astonishment and pleasure that came over me when I first read this proposal; but even the most sanguine backer of MacKaye's idea could hardly have guessed that this was such an idée-force — to use a French term — that Mac-Kaye would live to see the trail itself and some of the park area, as in the Great Smokies, finished before another twenty years had passed. The idea of long-distance trails had first been implanted in MacKaye in 1897, when, at the age of eighteen, he took a six-week walking trip with Sturgis Pray and a couple of other young fellows, in the White Mountains of New Hampshire. Much of the White Mountains then was still "forest primeval," and

MacKaye looks back to that trip now as the "toughest and greatest trip" of his whole life. Sturgis Pray was himself an inveterate trail-maker; and another scouting expedition that MacKaye made with him in 1903 showed MacKaye the value of long-distance trails. By dramatizing the long trail as the key to the Appalachian Empire, as he loved to call it, MacKaye incited hundreds of others to participate in the laying out of the route, achieving by purely voluntary cooperation and love what the empire of the Incas had done in the Andes by compulsory organization.

Through this article, and his friendship with Whitaker, MacKaye became acquainted with a new circle in New York, that which was brought into focus by the architect and planner, Clarence Stein, and formed the small select body that incorporated itself in 1923 as the Regional Planning Association of America — not to be confused with the heavily endowed metropolis-oriented Regional Plan Association of New York. A little before this association was formed I first met MacKaye; and for the rest of the decade our association was a particularly close one. Since I have already told something about the activities of this circle in my introduction to *New Towns for America,* by Clarence Stein, I shall not try to characterize their work and influence here, except to say that MacKaye's activities, MacKaye's ideas, and above all, MacKaye's generosity of spirit played a decisive part in all our work, modifying our city-minded approach, enlarging our horizons, and bringing into our lives the voice and touch of an older America, the America of the Eastern wilderness and the Western frontier: a heritage that we ignore at our peril.

MacKaye's regional planning studies for the New York State Housing and Regional Planning Commission brought out the contrast between the planning of small-scale communities on the older, self-sufficient pattern, and the planning of modern communities, where autonomy and balance must be achieved within a network of much wider cooperations. This work came to a head in MacKaye's outline of the "Regional Planning" number of the *Survey Graphic* magazine (May 1925): a survey of the problems and the hopes of regional planning that may one day take its place as a classic document. That number had been conceived by MacKaye and Robert Bruere, one of the *Survey Graphic* editors;

and while I undertook the editorial supervision, the main credit belongs to MacKaye — though I must add that our little group was so closely knit together by both our friendship and our common ends that the apportionment of credits or priorities never crossed our minds, for friends, as Socrates observed in *The Republic*, share all things together.

I do not propose here to follow through the rest of Benton MacKaye's life. My purpose has rather been to supply enough biographic data to explain the origins of *The New Exploration*, and to suggest what manner of man wrote this book, and what currents of thought and experience flowed into it. Physically, MacKaye is the archetypal Yankee, tall, lean, wiry, tough; and the thatch of black hair on his head, now white, is still thick: a man built to the measure of a Natty Bumppo or an Emerson, an Uncle Sam without the whiskers, with a touch of the Indian, or more likely the Highland Scot, in his saturnine features. MacKaye is a great man for both indoor and outdoor parties; he knows the secret of successful feasts, even with limited supplies: "Serve the food hot and have plenty of coffee." His talk is full of racy words and figures of speech, pungent with the smoke of many a campfire: "crazy as a bedbug," "wild as a loon," "hell on wheels," "Belshazzar feast." And he shares the family gift, with his father and his brother Percy, for mimicry and dramatization. To my grief, I could not be present at the pageant he organized in 1953 to celebrate the two hundredth anniversary of the town of Shirley; but by all reports it was a masterly performance, with MacKaye himself as director.

Fortunately, I have witnessed the care and craftsmanship he brought to many other such occasions; for it was he who first got our Regional Planning group reviving the country dances and singing the old New England songs, back in 1923, well before this folk revival had taken on generally. I know no one who has a better appreciation of the fine sociabilities of life: a good conversation, a good dinner, or a good theatrical performance; yet I know no one who is more capable of going without them with so little sense of loss, as he used to do when he was "batching it" in his old house in Shirley, in quarters that for sheer bareness and seediness would make most monastic cells look palatial. This combination of sociability and self-reliance, of urbanity and indigenous pernicketiness, of neighborliness and independence, is very much in the New England grain; and along with Robert Frost, one might be tempted to characterize him as the last of the old New England Yankees, were I not sure that another batch, just as characterful, is coming along, temporarily disguised by French, Polish, Italian, and Irish names.

So much for the man. But in passing to *The New Exploration* I must record one more trait that throws a light on MacKaye's genial character. In 1923, he had met Patrick Geddes; and in the course of two full days alone with him at the Hudson Guild Farm, had been delighted by Geddes's description of MacKaye's various activities as examples of "geotechnics," a term Geddes had coined for the arts of modeling and transforming the earth. In the original manuscript of *The New Exploration,* he had used this term, and wanted to put it in the subtitle as well. As an intermediary with the publisher, I foolishly thought that the book would have enough difficulty in getting accepted without the instrusion of this new term; and I persuaded him to change it to our more usual if not more self-explanatory term, "regional planning." Long after, MacKaye discovered, to his delight, that "geotechnics" had officially entered the dictionary; but by that time he had completely forgotten my officious interference with his early use of it. Let the reader correct my error by taking this book as a study in geotechnics!

When *The New Exploration* appeared in 1928, it was almost the only American book to handle such a broad subject, apart from the report done under Henry Wright for the State of New York; in fact most people were not even aware that such an art as geotechnics or regional planning was in existence even as an idea, or was partly visible as a fact without this label. There had long been an active school of French regional geographers, followed by their colleagues in Great Britain; and Peter Kropotkin's *Fields, Factories, and Workshops* had shown a thorough grasp of the new potentialities for rural and urban settlement, as widened by science and technics. But apart from Patrick Abercrombie's concrete plans for the development of Doncaster and similar regional areas, there were few precedents for the kind of philosophy and practice that MacKaye here undertook to expound. The work of Howard Odum, Rupert Vance, and their followers in the South was still to come.

From boyhood on, MacKaye had been fascinated by the major efforts at terrestrial exploration: the penetration of the uncharted wilderness beyond the known boundaries, as the prelude to their colonization and culture. In his new book, he turned this early pattern of exploration inside out, as it were, by applying the same general approach to exploring the "wilderness of industrial civilization," as concentrated in the great metropolitan areas. Here was another kind of unknown territory, another kind of barbarism. He beheld a machine-made fabric, increasingly standardized, regimented, characterless, spreading outward from the metropolis by a process seemingly as automatic as the spread of grassland, forest, and jungle in nature, breaking down the indigenous patterns of life, and removing even the valuable kind of variety that cosmopolitan contacts bring into every genuine city. I have belatedly coined the adjective "urbanoid" to designate this formless, low-grade, depolarized urban tissue, without an effective center or a visible boundary; but MacKaye first adequately described its operation.

Far more alert to what was going on than most of his contemporaries, MacKaye realized that this breakdown of an indigenous regional culture would in time also rob the metropolitan centers themselves of the environmental and human resources necessary for their own continued development. In no sense was his concern for the primeval and the rural a mere sentimental "back-to-nature" movement; still less was it an attack on the city. But unlike those who see no value in environmental variety, and no organic limits to the growth and spread of population, MacKaye had the intelligence to realize that "a city, to be an individual, must first of all have unity: to be an interesting individual, it must to some extent be cosmopolitan. These seem to be the two bedrock essentials of the true urban environment."

The tendency of the present-day exodus to suburbia is to bulldoze out of existence every evidence of variety and individuality in both the landscape and in human communities: the uncontrolled flow of population into ever more distant areas of the conurbation results in the coalescence of ever larger and looser urbanoid masses, a thinly spread conglomeration of homes, shopping centers, and factory sites adrift in a vast sea of car parks, whose planless existence provides excuse for the constantly multiplying expressways and cloverleafs and space-eating traffic interchanges that absorb, for the exaggerated needs of transportation, the time, the energy, the money, and the human effort that should go into more significant aspects of life.

Long before these tendencies had reached their present pinnacle of futility and frustration, MacKaye had foreseen the inevitable results: he realized that the "metropolitan invasion" would bring about a general surrender of human values which would in turn undermine the genuine values of the metropolis itself: the loss of any inner cohesion would leave it increasingly without the means to draw to itself the rich and varied resources, regional, inter-regional, and planetary, upon which the culture of cities has always depended. MacKaye emphasized that the "city is the first victim of the metropolitan flood." Now that the urban sprawl MacKaye pictured has effaced hundreds of square miles of the earth, once differentiated by both nature and man, one may add one other observation; and that is that the swollen metropolis itself, no less than the smaller cities it submerges, eventually becomes depleted at the center, through congestion and paralysis, just as it becomes emptied of its nighttime population by the endless suburban sprawl it promotes.

MacKaye's analysis of the process of metropolitan flow is an original contribution; likewise important was his description of the forces accelerating or retarding this flow: the local bottleneck, the threat of war, the economic struggle between capitalist and labor groups, and finally, the uprising of indigenous cultures. Let me underline this last item. What other planner was suggesting in 1928 that "the invasion of metropolitanism is perhaps about to meet an indigenous force which, light in iron, but heavy in man power and national tradition, may turn out to be an invincible opposition to what has appeared to be an irresistible flow." If MacKaye's kind of thinking had been more familiar in governmental circles, here and abroad, the great Colonial Powers might have used the decade that followed to plan an orderly retreat from Africa and Asia, instead of closing their eyes to the rising opposition, only to make the reluctant compromises and panicky flights that have, since 1945, characterized their response to the indigenous uprising.

MacKaye's more specific suggestions for controlling the metropolitan invasion, in terms of levees and dams, were a natural translation on his part of familiar wilderness terms to the new conditions for durable urban settlement; they have yet to be given a fair trial. But bold and comprehensive as many of MacKaye's proposals were in *The New Exploration,* he has not been satisfied merely to hold on to them; and I must say a word about his later contributions, which both validate and carry further the analysis he made in this book.

From this first broad outline of the problem, MacKaye went on, soon after the publication of *The New Exploration,* to deal with the design of the concrete means for controlling population flow. This took the form of a paper on "The Townless Highway," and a detailed study of the "Bay Circuit" around Boston, done for the Massachusetts Trustees of Reservations, a private body formed to acquire land by gift for public purposes. MacKaye's proposals for "The Townless Highway," originally published in *The New Republic* (30 March 1930), first put together in complete form all the components necessary for a fast motorway, before the highway engineers had yet visualized and carried to their logical conclusion the series of improvements that began with Frederick Law Olmsted's early parkway designs. Like the other members of his Regional Planning group, MacKaye fully grasped the role that the motor car would play in effecting a wide distribution of population; but unlike the highway engineers, he likewise understood that the new form of locomotion not merely demanded surface improvements in the old road system, but a radically different form of highway, which would have neither the time limitations of the horse-and-buggy age, nor the spatial limitations of the railroad age, with its linear system of distribution and its gutting out of the centers of cities for wasteful railroad yards (parking lots).

Thirty years ago MacKaye saw clearly that the necessary complement to the townless highway was the highwayless town: a new kind of town, first designed on a small scale by his friends Clarence Stein and Henry Wright, in Radburn, New Jersey, which insulated through traffic from the local traffic or the neighborhood, and would, carried further, separate the town itself from the major highways that would feed into it at intervals and yet bypass it. As yet, the highway engineers, with billions of dollars of public monies to command, have not caught up with MacKaye; instead, they have blindly, too often highhandedly and self-righteously, repeated all the flagrant errors made by their predecessors, the railroad engineers: in the name of theoretic speed and "progress" they butcher precious agricultural land to provide elaborately wasteful and often quite unnecessary local interchanges; they thrust expressways into rural areas that should be safeguarded against the haphazard and premature settlement that they actually encourage; they bulldoze their way into the hearts of towns and cities they should have bypassed by a generous margin; and in our bigger metropolitan centers, by wrecking the complex system of public transportation that existed even a generation ago, they destroy the centers of cities, turning potential parks into parking lots, and civic centers into garages, creating bottlenecks and traffic jams which slow down the sixty miles an hour achieved in the open country to a creeping six miles, or less, during the rush hour.

If our public officials and citizens had pondered MacKaye's analysis of "The Townless Highway," we should not merely have a more efficient and economic transportation system today; but many cities whose essential parts have been amputated and eviscerated, almost beyond surgical repair, would still be in a healthy condition, with all their necessary organs intact.

Were any further demonstration of MacKaye's insight and foresight in the field of environmental design needed, a contrast of his proposals for the Bay Circuit with the actual highway plan as carried out will admirably serve. Long before the highway engineers, MacKaye saw the necessity for a motor bypass around the ring of suburbs which encircle Boston, in order to make every part of the metropolitan area accessible, and yet to provide a swift through route which would make more accessible the north and the south shore towns and recreation areas, by wholly avoiding the dense urban settlements between. He visualized this circuit not as a mere motorway, but as a wide recreation belt: this belt would embrace a northbound motor road along the inner flank, and a southbound road along the outer flank, the two roads separated, not by the now usual strip, but by a wide band of usable green park, with footpaths and bicycle paths for recreational use.

This plan (see the *Boston Globe,* 31 Oct. 1930) was rejected by the so-called practical engineers and administrators in favor of a single-purpose motorway, Route 128. Because it neither provided for the public control of areas adjacent to the highway, nor set aside recreation space for the benefit of the whole metropolitan area, this route has become the site of an industrial and suburban development that is further depleting the central business area of Boston and, by the heavy load of traffic industry throws upon the expressway during the rush hours, is already making a mockery of the very purpose which this road was supposed specially to serve: fast transportation, guaranteed by its bypassing all dense clots of population. Instead of MacKaye's efficient greenbelt, the Bay Circuit is becoming a typical disorderly and inefficient motor slum: the standard pattern of "progress" from Los Angeles and San Francisco to Washington and Boston.

When one contrasts Benton MacKaye's timely analyses and forecasts with the shortsighted, single-factor analysis that passes for sound judgment in so many circles of government and business today, it is easy to see how visionary, in the worst sense of the word — that is, self-deluded — the practical men have been, and how shrewd and practical this Yankee visionary has been. If some of the data and illustrations for *The New Exploration* are no longer applicable, the philosophy behind it, and all the salient points of the main theses, are as fresh as they ever were: they still present a cogent basis for action. The present-day reader who follows MacKaye's trail-blazing in *The New Exploration* will have fresh insight, not merely into what has so disastrously happened to our environment in the last generation, but into what is still happening, abetted by extravagant federal subsidies — though happily against a rising murmur of protest. Best of all, the reader will have a glimpse of what may still take place, to undo this damage and to recultivate the blasted and blighted areas around us, if we bring to the task some of the hard-core courage, human sensibility, and socially alert "worry" that Benton MacKaye has brought to the "Expedition Nine" of his life.

LEWIS MUMFORD

Amenia, New York

PREFACE

This book is the direct result of my own work in regional planning during the past seven years. This work has been associated with a number of events and persons.

Through my friend Mr. Charles Harris Whitaker, editor of the *Journal* of the American Institute of Architects, I was enabled to launch my first project in this new field. The *Journal* for October, 1921, contained an article by me entitled "An Appalachian Trail: A Project in Regional Planning." This outlined the possibility of combining the various efforts of trail-building in the eastern mountain country so as to effect a continuous wilderness foot-path along the Appalachian Mountain Range from Maine to Georgia, such super-trail being conceived as a backbone on which to build a series of public forests, parks, and open ways. Since 1921 the work on this proposal has steadily advanced, and today most of the trail sections have been completed through New England, New York, New Jersey, eastern Pennsylvania, northern Virginia, and the Carolina mountains.

In March, 1925, the first Appalachian Trail Conference was held in Washington. This marked the second major step in the project — the selecting of a Committee of Fifteen representing all appropriate interests from New England to the Carolinas, to take general charge of the work. The committee was headed by Major William A. Welch, manager of the Palisades Interstate Park.

In April, 1923, the Regional Planning Association of America was organized in New York City. Mr. Alexander M. Bing of New York was chosen chairman of the executive committee. Mr. Bing, the prime mover in this country in the advancement of garden cities, has become well known through his activities as head of the City Housing Corporation and as the promoter of the projected city of Radburn in New Jersey. As a supporter of regional planning in America, through the Association and otherwise, and as a writer on its problems, Mr. Bing stands as a leading contributor to the movement. The Association has undertaken a number of studies on regional planning, including a report by the author on suggested approaches to its practice, and an agricultural plan for the Russian Reconstruction Farms, Inc.

In June, 1924, Mr. Clarence S. Stein, chairman of the New York State Commission of Housing and Regional Planning, asked me to undertake an outline for a survey looking to an ultimate State-wide plan for New York. This plan was afterward developed by Mr. Henry Wright, was admirably illustrated by him in a long series of maps and charts, and was published as a Report by the Commission to the Governor in 1926. The initiation of this report, however, does not mark my first association with Mr. Stein. In every project in regional planning since 1921 he has been in some way associated with me — often as chief or advisor, always as constructive helper.

The date of May, 1925, marks a milestone in the history of America's planning movement. The May issue of the *Survey Graphic* was brought out as a special Regional Planning Number. This consisted of a series of articles touching all salient phases of the subject, written by a group of specialists, including Alexander M. Bing, Clarence S. Stein, Henry Wright, Stuart Chase, Lewis Mumford, J. K. Hart, and Robert W. Bruère. Mr. Chase, writing on transportation, approached the planning question with his keen insight into national waste. Mr. Bruère brought to the subject his extensive background on matters of national giant-power. Mr. Bruère, as a member of the *Survey Graphic* staff, was the original proposer of the Regional Planning Number.

The latest project, which has had its influence upon the present book, is the one on which I have been recently engaged in the State of Massachusetts. This work has been done for the Governor's Committee on the Needs and Uses of Open Spaces: it looks to the control of the metropolitan flood through a system of open ways as described in Chapter XII.

This book quotes voluminously from Henry David Thoreau. This is not merely because Thoreau is a favorite of the present author. It is because, in the author's opinion, the notes and com-

ments of this seer on the simple potencies of life and life's environment form the fragments (the precious stones, if you please) for
building some day a structure of philosophy for remolding human
outlooks on the earth. Thoreau is the philosopher of environment:
he saw the eternities of the indigenous, and he foresaw the inroad-
ings of the metropolitan.

This book also quotes frequently from a contemporary writer —
Mr. Lewis Mumford. This is not simply the bias of a friend. It
is because in certain of his writings, and especially in his book,
The Golden Day, Mr. Mumford combines ideas of cultural and
geographic significance which seem to place him among classic
writers on environment and among the revealers of our innate
indigenous world.

To other writers — to other friends who have given generously
of their time and spirit in encouraging this work, and in criticizing
the manuscript, go my keen appreciation and my enduring
thoughts.

BENTON MACKAYE

Shirley Center
Massachusetts
August 15, 1928

CONTENTS

MAPS

THE NEW EXPLORATION

Chapter I

LONDON BRIDGE AND TIMES SQUARE

No spot in the world is better known than London, and no spot in London is better known than London Bridge. Let the reader suppose that he is standing upon this bridge, and, heedless of the passing stream of traffic, looks down upon the river as it runs below.

With these words Huxley opens one of his works on "An Introduction to the Study of Nature." He describes the ebb and flow of the tide in the Thames under London Bridge and queries as to the ultimate source and cause of this great force. He traces for us the river back to its headwaters in the Cotteswold Hills; he then traces the river's sources to the springs which feed the headwaters, to the rains which feed the springs, and to the ocean whence the rain water is derived. He traces the winds and the atmospheric behavior whereby the waters are carried from the oceans to the lands. He traces the behavior of the eternal land itself, its erosion and its uplifts, and shows the reason for the hills and dales whose solid substance constitutes the territory of the Thames basin. He goes even further: to that cosmic body whose radiating energy appears as the ultimate outward cause of these land and water and atmospheric movements; and he closes his exploration with this paragraph:

And thus we reach, at last, the goal of our inquiry. At the furthest point to which we have pushed our analysis . . . the sun is revealed as the grand prime mover in all that circulation of matter which goes on . . . within the basin of the Thames; and the spectacle of the ebb and flow of the tide, under London Bridge, from which we started, proves to be a symbol of the working of forces which extend from planet to planet, and from star to star, throughout the universe.

Here is a goal indeed—the revelation of the prime mover in our earth's material affairs! But note how the author modifies his revelation: "at the furthest point to which we have pushed our analysis"; for nobody knew better than Huxley that the full comprehension of those forces which extend throughout the universe is the subject of an everlasting quest, and that the proximate understanding which we thus far have attained is indeed but an "introduction" to the vast study of nature.

This introduction marks the end of a beginning. It marks a coming of age in human comprehension. We have reached a definite milestone. Physically, at all events, we begin to see ourselves within the universe: we find ourselves afloat (but not adrift) on a symmetrical body moving under articulate law in coöperative rhythm with other cosmic bodies; we find ourselves also in the vanguard of a biologic evolution whose lowly origins give promise of transcendent goals. The revelations which were first focused in Copernicus and Darwin are tangible truths or probabilities in the realm of universal exploration comparable with the revelations of da Gama, Columbus, and Magellan, in the realm of terrestrial exploration.

The exploration of the outstanding wilderness of nature has now gone into history. The unveiling of its guiding law, from Archimedes to Newton, from Aristotle to Darwin, and its revelation as a fact, from Marco Polo to Peary and Amundsen, have now taken their permanent places in the world's accomplishments. Nature's mystery has in good part been penetrated—and her domain conquered. But alas! The very conquering of one wilderness has been the weaving of another. Mankind has cleared the jungle and replaced it by a labyrinth. Through the sudden potent operation of the industrial revolution a maze of iron bands has now been spun around the earth; this forms the modern labyrinth of "industrial civilization." And the unraveling of this tangled web is the problem of our day.

This "unraveling" will require an exploration more complicated perhaps (though probably less lengthy) than that required to unfold the continental wildernesses themselves and the causes of the ebb and flow of water under London Bridge. Huxley, in order to present a bird's-eye view of his problem, takes us to this Bridge and asks us to note the flow of the waters taking place thereunder. We shall now adapt his method to our own problem, but instead of going to London Bridge we shall go to Times Square. Let us paraphrase his words:

No spot in America is better known than New York, and no spot in New York is better known than Times Square. Let the reader suppose that he is standing on top of the Times Building, and, heedless of the passing Hudson River, looks down upon the stream of traffic as it runs below.

The reader is asked by Huxley to be "heedless of the passing stream of traffic" and to direct his attention upon the "river." The reader now is asked to be *heedless of the passing river* and to direct his attention upon the *stream of traffic.*

Well, let us look into this stream of traffic. Let us go to
the bottom of it—push aboard the elevator and drop down
into the subway. Anybody who has ever been in the Times
Square station of the subway knows that he has struck a

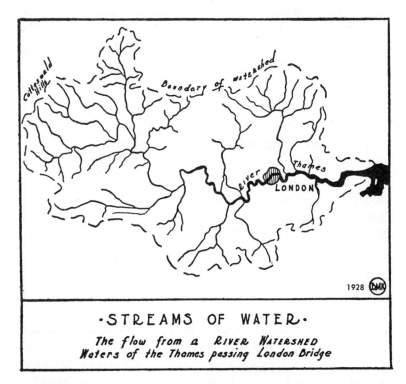

· S T R E A M S   O F   W A T E R ·

The flow from a RIVER WATERSHED
Waters of the Thames passing London Bridge

"stream." Follow the green lights to the West Side trains,
or else the red lights to the Shuttle: go with the arrows; if
you try to go counter or to "strike across" you will have
about as much chance as a decrepit swimmer in the
gorge below Niagara. Two-thirds of this stream is made up
of that product of metropolitanism known as the *commuter*, a somewhat human species which, to quote the

press, is carried each day "from places where they would rather not live to places where they would rather not work, and back again." Two million of the three million day-time population of lower Manhattan flow into that

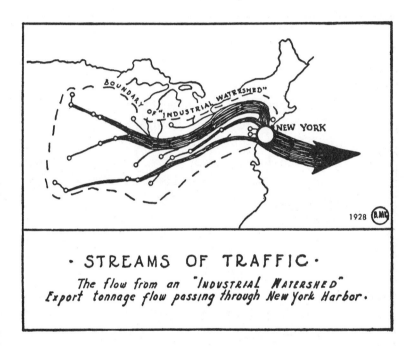

· STREAMS OF TRAFFIC ·

The flow from an "INDUSTRIAL WATERSHED"
Export tonnage flow passing through New York Harbor ·

section and out again each day. This stream, therefore, can be readily analyzed: it consists of folks and not of freight; it is a tidal flow rather than a river, the two periods of high water being reached about 8 A.M. and 5 P.M. The minor portion of the stream consists of shoppers, theater-goers, job-hunters, errand boys, loafers, and befuddled humanity generally, these forming a daytime low-water current which rises to a slight tide of theater commuters along toward midnight.

Let us step upstairs into the street—at the corner of Broadway and Forty-second Street and Seventh Avenue. Here the stream is more complex; that is to say, there is more than one stream. There is still the stream of folks— on the sidewalks, in the surface cars, in the taxicabs. First it rushes north and south, clanging, honking, and otherwise shrieking as it goes; then the policeman's whistle blows, and the stream shoots east and west.

In addition to this there is another kind of stream, though one less evident. There must be one, or how could the shop windows be so full of "things"? Yes, there is a stream of *things* as well as of folks. It consists of auto-trucks, and even horse-drawn drays. These trucks are bringing ladies' shoes to Macy's; they are bringing sealing-wax to the corner stationer's—and cabbages to the corner grocery. They bring moth balls to Liggett's, candies to the United Cigars, and heaven knows what to Woolworth's. Where do the trucks pick up this stuff? At the freight yards and the water fronts. And how comes it there? Ah, that is a big story. Where are the sources of all these streams of things? Here is a question perhaps as vast as the one that Huxley put—what are the sources of the River Thames?

Let us go back again to the top of the Times Building and get a wider view. What do we see? Less and more. The outstanding sight before us is a thing which is mentioned in the Century Dictionary: "a bewildering mass, heap or collection," which is one of the definitions of the word "wilderness." We see a cross-section of the wilderness of modern western mechanized civilization. It is grand to be-hold. At first glance it looks like a civilization of *shapes*— towers, windows, canyons, chimneys, grain elevators. Below on the street corner it seemed like a civilization of shapes and shrieks and motions. But from the heights the totality of shrieks has become a low current of roar, and the main motion evident is the reposeful drift of the ships in the harbor. By what we have seen from high and low we are reminded of *Through the Looking-Glass*.

"The time has come," the Walrus said, "to talk of many things:
  Of shoes and ships and sealing-wax—of cabbages and kings."

The walrus must have been talking about civilization. For what more magnificent chaos than that presented from the top and bottom of Times Square—the very heart of the American section of Western civilization! And yet what magnificent order in this magnificent chaos! From the scheduled arrival of the ocean liner to the sharp blast of the policeman's whistle and the delicate arrangement of the shoe-shop window! But what of order is there in this order?

Can we from the top of the Times Building trace aught of design in the various streams of traffic flowing into New York City? Yes, if we look closely. The stream of folks is a comparatively simple matter. We can see up into the Bronx and over into Long Island City and across into Jersey. There we can discern (perhaps we need a field glass) the suburban "massings of humanity," the circular fringe of tenements and clothes-lines marking the places where the commuters "would rather not live"; while nearer and all around us are seen the skyscrapers where they "would rather not work." The stream of commuter traffic entering the city is then readily visualized as a flow from suburb to skyscraper and back again. This much is easy. But what of the stream (or streams) of freight traffic entering the city? Whence come these streams? Where and what are the *sources* of our material existence?

It takes something stronger than a field glass to bring within our vision the sources whence arise the streams of various commodities which flow into New York. The field glass, to be sure, discloses to us the Hudson Highlands which mark the main ridge of the great Appalachian barrier, and it almost shows us where, between Bear Mountain and Anthony's Nose, the mighty Hudson itself pushes through and opens the only level highway into the continent's interior. But beyond this we shall need a greater instrument—the ability to visualize through the imagination the continent's interior itself. Training then our telescope of visualization in the right direction, we see the Dakota wheat farm as the prime source of a stream of breadstuffs which, converted into flour in Minneapolis, flows through Chicago and over the N.Y.C. lines through Buffalo and Albany into the warehouses on Manhattan Island. Another view discloses a cattle ranch in western Kansas as the source of a stream which, starting as cattle on the hoof, is converted at St. Louis into beef, and then flows over the Pennsylvania lines into Jersey City. In a similar way one sees a stream of cotton goods starting in a Georgia cotton field, a stream of iron ore rising in the Massaba Range in Minnesota and flowing by way of the Great Lakes to Cleveland and thence to Pittsburgh, where, joined by a stream of coal from a West Virginia mine, it is converted first into steel and next into girders, and then flows on to New York to be set up into modern buildings. Thus, roughly speaking, are New York's commuters fed and clothed and sheltered in return for their "pen driving" in the skyscrapers.

New York City, from this further look through the field glass of the imagination, appears now as a huge yawning, yearning mouth for the product of vast lands and regions within the American continent. But let us look again. What does that big freighter steaming out of the harbor mean? It is bound for a foreign port with a cargo of wheat and beef and iron goods from the sources we have named; it is a continuation of the streams which we have already traced to the continent's edge. Again directing our imagination, we visualize the 22 per cent. of America's export tonnage which squeezes through the Port of New York to flow to England, to Italy, to Cape Town, to Buenos Aires, to Shanghai (via Panama), and to the other seaports of the world.

Thus our view from the Times Building becomes more and more distinct. New York at first is a blur—a "bewildering mass." Next, through better focusing, it is visualized as the ultimate mouth of extensive interior regions. Finally it is revealed as a mutinous whirlpool of converging and diverging streams whose sources lie within the continent and whose mouths lie not alone in the city itself but in the ports and centers scattered throughout the world.

New York is what is known as a *metropolis*—a "mother of cities." More accurately it is a mother of traffic streams, a place where they are taken under one wing and allowed to sputter and bubble in concert. But New York is only one: there are nearly thirty other centers in the United States listed by the Census as "metropolitan districts." There is Chicago, toward the center of the continent; there is San Francisco, gateway to the Pacific Coast; there is Boston on the Atlantic, and Detroit, Cleveland, Philadelphia, Baltimore, Washington. There are several lesser ones, twenty-nine in all with a central population of

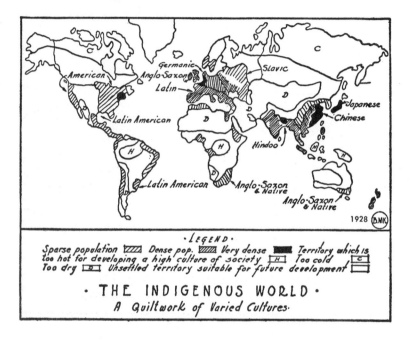

·LEGEND·
Sparse population 🔲 Dense pop. 🔲 Very dense ▬ Territory which is too hot for developing a high culture of society 🔲 Too cold 🔲 Too dry 🔲 Unsettled territory suitable for future development 🔲

· THE INDIGENOUS WORLD ·
A Quiltwork of Varied Cultures·

200,000 or over. Any major conflux of traffic streams is for our purposes a metropolis—big or little. And they are riveted together by bands of steel, or of concrete. Every railway and every motor-road is a metropolitan highway. New York, therefore, is but one metropolis in America's metropolitan framework.

Europe also has its metropolitan framework. This is linked with America's by a series of steamship lines. Together these frameworks form the nucleus of Western civilization—modern iron metropolitan civilization. Its iron tentacles, in the form of steamships and ocean cables and battle cruisers, have been reaching into other portions of the world. It has set up frameworks in Argentina, in South

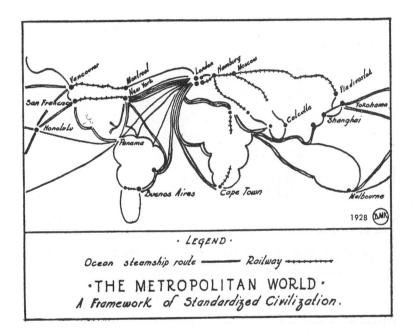

· LEGEND ·

Ocean steamship route ——— Railway · · · · · · ·

·THE METROPOLITAN WORLD·
A Framework of Standardized Civilization.

Africa, and in Australia. It has made its beginning in the East; entrances have been forced through Bombay and Calcutta, and through Hongkong and Shanghai.

So the immediate view from the Times Building—the peaks and canyons of Manhattan Island—is a view also of Chicago and Boston and San Francisco; of Liverpool and Hamburg; of Buenos Aires and Cape Town and Melbourne; as well as of the dreamed-for Singapore, Madras, and Peking. It is a cross-section of metropolitan civilization the world over, the triumphant realization of Manhattan and the dream of Main Street. "The only place where I ever saw the streets of Cairo," writes a friend of mine from those very streets, "was at the Chicago Fair in 1893, for the flivver here has now replaced the camel." So look upon Manhattan and behold the coming world.

But no—only half of it. Look over yonder there at the Hudson Highlands (you do not even need your field glasses). In those hills there lives a man who recently made his first visit to New York. He had lived a long life within fifty miles from Times Square, and in spite of the Sunday supplement had no real notion of a metropolis. Yonder in the Appalachian hinterland there dwells another world. This world is the indigenous America. It is being invaded (but is not yet captured) by metropolitan America. So indigenous China is not the only country being thus invaded.

In brief, we have discovered two worlds in surveying the landscape from the Times Building—just as Huxley discovered two worlds from London Bridge. Immediately beneath us, we observed the streams of traffic, passing through Manhattan, streams which flow and mingle with all the great traffic and goods streams of the earth. Here is the realm of the metropolis, the mouth that receives the industrial flow, the domain of standardized existence. It is a transient and ever-changing environment. In the hinterland of the great metropolis, we have visualized the industrial watershed, the parts of the country where the traffic streams take rise, first in small trickles and runnels, in farms, ranches, mines, forests, and then broadening into the vast streams of raw materials which go, as food or as basic products, into the homes and workshops of the world. Here is the realm of the indigenous, the realm of the soil, the ores, the forests, the water-power forces, and of the other sources of life and industry. If the metropolitan environment presents us typically with what flows and passes and changes, the indigenous environments provide us with what stays. A railway may stop running, or a city may disappear: but the earth itself, as a receiver and storer of solar energy, as a hoarder and container of soils and metals and potential vegetation—that does not alter: it can never basically alter.

The two worlds perceived from London Bridge were the subject for our great past explorations which led to the comprehension and control of the wilderness of nature. From the top of the Times Building we have seen two other worlds. They are the subject for the capital exploration of the future—the visualization of the wilderness of civilization, and the invention of ways and means for controlling and finally conquering it.

Chapter II

THE WILDERNESS OF CIVILIZATION

He: "What is civilization—is it having steam engines?"
She: "No, it is the development of our cultural possibilities."

This fragment of conversation I overheard one Sunday morning as I was seated in a Lackawanna Railroad car pulling out of Hoboken. Our own "steam engine" was snorting through the engine yards, and the rest of the cargo, we humans, went lumbering after it. We passed by a round house in front of which on a turnstile a glorious big engine stood jovially hissing in its reposeful power and blowing imperturbably through its single upturned nostril a long black column toward the sky. Then we passed another round house with cowcatchers peeping through the doorways. Next we were snorted around a curve in view of the Jersey meadows containing linear acres of freight cars with steam engines at each end. After some more snortings there appeared the April-tinted ridges of the Ramapos against the cloudless morning blue. The rumble blotted out the conversation of my neighbors, and so I pondered on the fragment I had heard.

They were a pleasant-looking couple, dressed in walking costume, bound apparently for a day's tramp on the heights overlooking our modern "Rome." Obviously they were using steam engines, and—as obviously—were bent on avoiding them. Indeed the very reason they were using them seemed to be in order to get as far away from them as possible. Had I been the lady answering the gentleman, I should have revised her reply thus:

"Sir, civilization (the bulk of it) consists verily in *having steam engines;* nine tenths of our life, alas, is used up in the *means* of life: but if now you will be so agreeable as to ask me what *ends* civilization is supposed to serve, then I say it is the development of man's *cultural possibilities.*"

Undoubtedly that was the object of these folks: they were spending their Sunday not to gaze on steam engines (sublime as these may be), but to develop their own cultural possibilities. To my mind they were going about it in the right way: they were going to the sources; they were not going to read about life, they were going to partake of it directly—under the heavens and above the world, and in company which compounded the day's adventure.

All this seems so simple: steam engines—the railroad—these are civilization's *means;* these are what we ride upon. Yet do we? Thoreau says, "We do not ride on the railroad; it rides upon us." He follows up this point. "Did you ever think," he writes, "what those sleepers are that underlie the railroad? Each one is a man, an Irishman, or a Yankee man. The rails are laid on them, and they are covered with sand, and the cars run smoothly over them."

If we check up this ghastly statement with recent engineering studies, we shall find that it is not far wrong. Mr. Stuart Chase, in his book *The Tragedy of Waste,* estimates that the working life of at least 20,500,000 American workers is wholly wasted. It is squandered, that is, in making useless stuff, or lost in enforced idleness, or frittered away in taking needless steps in the processes of industry. There are in the United States about 250,000 miles of railroad—a distance a little greater than that from the earth to the moon. There are about 2,600 railroad ties (or sleepers) per mile, making a total of 650,000,000 in the whole country. Dividing this number by the number of wasted American workers gives us 32. Thoreau, therefore, is wrong: not *every* sleeper is a man, but every 32 of them are. For every four rods of rail that we "run smoothly over" there is a man put away—"an Irishman, or a Yankee man," or some other kind of *man*—whose hard days of labor have contributed nothing to the real needs of mankind.

If the mechanism of American industry blots out the usefulness of twenty million lives (which is half the workers of the country), then surely "the railroad rides on us" and our civilization consists of "having steam engines." We doubt if the civilization of the Aztecs could have rendered such a grotesque account. But is it civilization, or the wilderness in which it is enmeshed, that makes us so grotesque?

Let us not be confused about this point: to see this paradox is not to decry engines or machines, for these are a part of nature. "The machine," says Mr. J. K. Hart, "is nature dressed up in modern clothes." We mean no harking back to "good old stage-coach days." But if we should peep back at them and join Thoreau on the shores of Walden Pond in 1845, we should hear some other thoughts of his about the railroad; and these at first glance appear to be quite different from the thoughts which we have quoted. Listen to him:

When I hear the iron horse make the hills echo with his snort like thunder . . . it seems as if the earth had got a race now worthy to inhabit it. If all were as it seems, and men made the elements their servants for noble ends!

I watch the passage of the morning cars with the same feeling that I do the rising of the sun, which is hardly more regular. . . . If the enterprise were as innocent as it is early! . . . as heroic and commanding as it is protracted and unwearied!

The startings and arrivals of the cars are now the epochs in the village day. They go and come with such regularity and precision . . . that the farmers set their clocks by them, and thus one well-conducted institution regulates a whole country.

Thoreau in these few sentences expresses his hopes and his doubts. Like every other great seer, he sees the promise and the menace in the sudden invention of an instrument of power. Modern industry is an electric switchtower in the hands of a five-year-old, and Thoreau had a hunch that this was so. The child can press a button and keep the coming train on the track (to go on its way to promised lands), or he can press a button and throw it in the ditch.

Thoreau sees the iron horse as a member of a race worthy to inhabit God's own earth; he revels in Nature, whether she is naked or whether she is "dressed up in modern clothes." He feels the lure we all have felt at the long, hoarse call of the engine's whistle across the dark night lands. An incidental strain in the drama of a continental growth, as if terrestrial evolution were being set to music! Which one of us as a boy has not aspired to work on the railroad? Personally I never was tempted to run away to sea, but I once confessed to a doting aunt my secret heart's ambition "to run away to land" (which meant to get a job as an Armstrong's news agent on the three o'clock express over the Hoosac Tunnel line).

"Thus one well-conducted institution," says Thoreau, "regulates a whole country." "I am refreshed and expanded," he says, "when the freight train rattles past me . . . reminding me of foreign parts, of coral reefs, and Indian oceans, and tropical climes, and the extent of the globe. I feel more like a citizen of the world." Here is the whole philosophy of world-integration. If an industrial framework (of which the railroad must long be the great coördinator) could inspire in the ordinary man such thoughts as these—to be "refreshed and expanded when the freight train rattles past"—it would form the medium for a new humanity. But—"if all were as it *seems,* and men made the elements their *servants* for noble ends!" Industry—servant or master?—that, of course, is the whole question. Will the framework which the genius of man has woven become a terrestrial lacework for the integration of his own terrestrial powers, or will it become a tangled net in which he will be strangled?

Such are Thoreau's hopes and fears for the railroad as the basis and symbol of on-rushing industry—will we ride on *it,* or will *it* ride on us? In 1845 his provisional conclusion was that it had *begun* anyhow to ride on us, and today we are conscious that the weight has increased rather than lessened.

The railroad has put a civilization on wheels. I say *a* civilization, because ours is only one. There are at present in this world at least two civilizations—the Eastern and the Western. The Western is very largely the product of the industrial or mechanical revolution. The railroad, since Thoreau's time eight decades ago, has put over a number of big "railway empires"—in North America, in Argentina, in South Africa, in Europe itself; and now it is beginning on Asia. In short, the world is being "railroaded"; and this is why the industrial labyrinth, of which the transportation system forms the underpinning, is the big outstanding material problem of the present generation.

But it is something more than a material problem. A civilization, like a man, seems to consist of three elements. Man, when boiled down to lowest terms, seems to consist of three things: his soul, his body, and his shirt. I speak not in jest: the shirt is a symbol and a sample of the artificially supplied, though inevitable needs of physical man. A civilization consists of the respective equivalents: the thoughts of men; the bodies of men; the material equipment or effects of men. The second element must always be present in a civilization—the men and women themselves as physical entities. For a civilization, therefore, of a given population, the fundamental question seems to relate to the relative proportion of elements one and three —to the ratio, so to speak, of men's thoughts to their material effects. Civilization's labyrinth, then, presents an outstanding problem in thought and culture, as well as a material difficulty.

Oswald Spengler, in his book *The Decline of the West,* if I understand him correctly, uses the word *culture* to designate the "thought element" which we have mentioned, while reserving the term *civilization* to designate the "material element." Lewis Mumford, in *The Golden Day,* refers to "civilization and culture, the material fact and the spiritual form." Keeping these distinctions in mind, the interesting theme which Spengler has worked out with regard to a possible cycle of "civilization" and "culture" is very significant in any approach to the unraveling of what we have called "the labyrinth of industrial civilization." Briefly, his theme is this:

Human society may be compared to a man: it goes through birth, youth, maturity, senility, and death. One human society is succeeded by another, just as one man's life is succeeded by another's. The period which in man is called *youth*, in human society is called *culture*—the period of creative growth and development. The period which in man is called *senility*, in human society is called *civilization*—the period of stagnation which precedes the end.

Human society may be compared also to the four seasons: it has its springtime, its summer, its autumn, and its winter. One human society is followed by another just as the four seasons are followed by another four. Culture starts in the springtime of a society, the age of conception and of re-creation—and then grows as does the maple sapling, on throughout the summer. Civilization begins in the autumn of a society, the age of the sear leaf and decay —and then extends as the glacier does in rigid expansion to the winter's end.

Cultures, according to Spengler, are "sublimated life-essences" which "grow with the same superb aimlessness as the flowers of the field." Cultures are detected by the arts. The fine arts are to a society what the sap and the biologic processes are to the oak tree. When in nature the November oak leaves wither and turn a tawdry brown, then we know life's processes have been suspended and that winter is at hand. When in a society the arts turn drab and strain at getting color through reproducing old effects, then we know the "life-essences" have ceased and that "civilization" is upon us. Spengler speaks of the Greek régime as a *culture* and of the Roman régime as a *civilization*. Thus, roughly speaking, we might say that the period leading up to Pericles and Aristotle in the fifth and fourth centuries B.C. was the "springtime" of the ancient Mediterranean society, while the period marked by the coming of the Goths and Vandals, in the fourth and fifth centuries after Christ, was the "winter" of that society.

According to Spengler we have now got around to another winter—"we" being Western European and American society. He sees this society as dominated by imperialism, which he calls "civilization unadulterated," and he picks Cecil Rhodes as the man of our particular hour. He describes Rhodes as "the first precursor of a Western type of Caesars, whose day is to come though yet distant. . . . His phrase, 'expansion is everything,' is the Napoleonic reassertion of the in-dwelling tendency of *every* civilization that has fully ripened."

Metropolitanism, along with imperialism, he cites as another sign of our "winter" season. Thus he says:

> In place of a world, there is a *city, a point,* in which the whole life of broad regions is collecting while the rest dries up. In place of a type-true people, born of and grown on the soil, there is a new sort of nomad, cohering unstably in fluid masses, the parasitical city-dweller, traditionless, utterly matter-of-fact, religionless, clever, unfruitful, deeply contemptuous of the countrymen. . . . This is a very great stride toward the inorganic, toward the end. . . .

Such is Herr Spengler's theme. If we accept it, as a working hypothesis, and if also we aspire, for ourselves or our immediate posterity, to the experience of a life of *culture* as against that of *civilization,* then we shall be discouraged or not, according to our expectation of a long "winter" or our hopes for an "early spring." Will it be years or decades or centuries? We know history to be a slow-moving affair, but there is one factor which should impel us to take any historical analysis with the regulation grain of salt. The unique event in world-history of the industrial revolution and our potentially impressive control over the "material fact" has, in a sense, the effect of calling off all prophecy. With the "railroading" process which has now commenced, what once took centuries may in the future require only decades. If the "spring" should promise to be "late" (within the next few centuries), then it does not seem to matter what we do just now in preparation for it. But if the industrial snows of "winter" should suddenly break up (perhaps within a generation) and thaw into a deluge, then we may well be looking for some ark in which to navigate. What manner of ark, what manner of makeshift world, might we effect in this emergency, on which to sojourn until such time as the sun of destiny can rise high enough in heaven to bring a full-fledged "spring"?

Here is a significant and decisive question for this generation. Can we make of this time and century something better than a chaos of industrial cross-purposes? We find ourselves in the shoes of our forefathers: their job was to unravel the wilderness of nature; ours is to unfold the wilderness of civilization. Or are we to be lost in the jungle of industrialism? Are the elements of water and steam and fire to remain our masters, or will they become our "servants for noble ends"? Are we going to ride on the railroad or let it ride on us? These questions promise to be answered one way or the other during the present century. The answer depends, for one thing, on our ability to comprehend the old and new forces that surround us. What can we learn from the comprehenders, the explorers, the guides, of the past?

Chapter III

EXPLORATION—OLD AND NEW

We have taken two looks at civilization. We have looked
upon it through our own physical eyes from Times Square
and seen it as a flowing stream of traffic, having its sources
in a continental hinterland and its ultimate "mouths" in
the peopled centers throughout the world. We have looked
upon it also through the eyes of the philosopher and the
historian and have seen it as a creeping labyrinth, a wiring
and railroading of the world, an iron cobwebbing in the
winter of a human cycle. Through both sets of eyes we see
it as a colossal, headless, almost cosmic process of "getting ready to live." How, then, about the *living* itself?
This is the question that confronted the explorers of the
past in coping with the wilderness of nature, and it is the
question which confronts the explorers of the future in
coping with the wilderness of civilization. Again we ask—
what lessons can we learn from our elder comprehenders
of the world?

We have cited the river—the stream of water—as the
key to the old exploration. MacKenzie, the first man to
cross North America, went with a canoe. LaSalle, when
he laid out the erstwhile empire of New France, followed
the labyrinth of Mississippi tributaries until he reached
the destination of that continental system. The prairie
lands enclosed within the meshes of this system were to

26

form the seat of a projected civilization; and this came to pass, but, through the strange antics of fate, not in the way LaSalle had planned. The river valley is the natural seat of a civilization. It was by way of the river that men were first led to their particular seat of settled life, and it was by means of the river's flow that the area was made to serve men's needs. The river has been man's faithful ally in reducing the wilderness of nature, and thereby indirectly in enabling him to spread the wilderness of civilization.

The oldest civilizations were river civilizations—on the Nile, the Euphrates, the Ganges, the Hwang-ho. The river as a unifying factor laid the physical foundation of each state. The integrated society of Egypt was in strong contrast with the scattered nomad society of the adjoining Sahara. The Nile was an integrator in more ways than one—as a highway, as a replenisher of soil fertility, and as the source of a bountiful supply of water for agricultural crops and for sanitation purposes. Abundance of water meant abundance in other ways; scarcity of water meant scarcity in other ways. The Egyptians lived and thrived on the flood plain of the Nile, while the Sahara nomads wandered from one water-hole to another.

The conquering of nature's wilderness and the installing of civilization was a matter, therefore, of exploring for supplies of water, quite as much as for supplies of land. The river generally was a guide to both, for it usually spelled rainfall and also level lands for cultivation. *Land* and *water*—each of these elements is, of course, as fundamental as the other; but *air* or atmosphere is in a sense more vital than either—air not only as air, but as the medium of rainfall and salubrious temperature. So the "old exploration" embraced all three of the geographic elements—the lands, the waters, and the atmosphere.

Some close parallels are followed by the old exploration and the new. The river or water stream is the guide to the *terra incognita* of the continent; the traffic or commodity stream is the guide to the *terra incognita* of industrial civilization. Each stream traverses the full length of a wilderness; each stream connects the visible sources of a world-circulation with their visible destinations. The new exploration has its own equivalent for land, water-flow, and atmosphere: these are natural resources, commodity-flow, and environment. Let us take a look at this second trio.

The relation of land to natural resources is fairly obvious, also the relation of water-flow to commodity-flow; these need no elaboration: but the paralleling of the remaining elements is perhaps not quite so plain. How does environment correspond to "atmosphere"? We cannot answer this question adequately without considering what we mean by environment.

The primary necessities of man are usually given as "food, clothing, and shelter." With the birds it is different; all they must get for themselves is food. Food supplies the robin with his body and his feathered "shirt," since all he needs for physical shelter, except at nesting-time, is the twig of some sheltering tree. Between the worm and the tree he is provided with the wherewithal for developing all three of his parts—his body, his "shirt," and his little soul. (These you will remember as the three elements also of mankind—the soul, the body, and the "shirt.") Cock robin needs only the worm and the tree, but man requires food and clothing and houses and "things." But even then he has not enough: these are sufficient for his body and his "shirt," but how about his soul?

A house alone is not sufficient for a soul, even when heated and lighted and kitchened and bath-roomed. Neither is furniture, nor equipment—even to the nth power of household effects. It takes more than these to make a home. Likewise it takes more than houses and streets and sewers to make a real community. It takes more than towns and railroads and corn fields to make a nation and a pleasant land to live in. These are enough for the "material fact," but not for the "spiritual form." They are enough for a mechanical state of "civilization," but not for a living "culture." Man needs more than this to cover God's green earth if he would be a *soul*. He needs just one thing further. He needs it in his home and dooryard; he needs it within his community; he needs it throughout his country and his planet. It is the right kind of *environment*.

Environment is to the would-be cultured man what air is to the animal—it is the breath of life. So far as outward matters go, environment is the basic ingredient of living as air is of existence.

Here, then, we have the fields of the old exploration and the new: the outward needs of man engaged merely in a material struggle, and those of cultured man. Pioneer man needs land as the tangible source of bodily existence; he needs the flow of waters to make that source effective; but above all, he needs air as the constant source and revivifier of his activity. Cultured man needs land and developed natural resources as the tangible source of bodily existence; he needs the flow of commodities to make that source effective; but first of all he needs a harmonious and related environment as the source of his true living.

These three needs of cultured man make three corresponding problems:

(a) The conservation of natural resources.

(b) The control of commodity-flow.

(c) The development of environment.

The visualization of the potential workings of these three processes constitutes the new exploration—and regional planning.

The essentials of the old exploration were *actualities;* the essentials of the new exploration are *potentialities.* The old exploration described *that which is,* while the new exploration projects *that which can be.* The first was based on descriptive science; the second is based on applied science. The one was a recording of actual facts and of nature's laws; the other is a charting of possible facts lying within those laws. The workers in each exploration have consisted (or consist) of two types: the searchers for the law or principle involved, and the searchers for the fact or potentiality.

One type of worker in the *old exploration* was the *man of science.* We have already cited Huxley. The man of science sought the laws of nature. He sought the causes of her outward facts: the causes—proximate and ultimate —of the ebb and flow of waters under London Bridge. He sought these causes in the erosion and the carving of the lands, in the uplifting of continents, in the circulation of the waters from springs to ocean and from ocean to springs, in the circulation of the winds, in the rotation of the earth on its axis, and in the radiation from our final source of energy in the sun. To Huxley's masterly review of this great quest we have already referred. The man of science followed also the complex thread of causes through our planetary life (in plant and animal kingdoms) and arrived at the great law of evolution. And thus through the giant efforts of such men as Aristotle, Galileo, Copernicus, Cuvier, and Darwin, we have come through the first stage in our everlasting pursuit of the mysteries of nature's universe.

The other type of worker in the old exploration was the *explorer* himself, who, because his exploits are more readily visualized than those of his co-worker, has given the name to the quest itself of unraveling the mystery and wilderness of terrestrial nature. The explorer sought not the laws but the facts of nature, and only some of these. He sought the outward, the geographic facts—first the locations of the continents, and then, through the guiding rivers, the condition of the interior land-masses. The unveiling of the continents, outside and in, has been a matter of relatively recent times. The travels of Marco Polo, which started in 1271, initiated the contact between the Western and the Eastern mind, but no *new* countries were discovered until the fifteenth century, when the march of Portuguese ships took place down the west coast of Africa. At this time, writes Mr. H. S. Hildebrand in his book *Magellan,* history "became a sudden stream of purpose. The world awoke—and started"; it "was ready for three great navigators": Vasco da Gama, Christopher Columbus, and Ferdinand Magellan. Between these three men, in one instant of history (1487 to 1521), the geographic world was broken open: it remained for Sir Francis Drake and Captain Cook to follow them in locating the main coast-lines; for the

Orellanas and the LaSalles and the Stanleys to delve into the continents; and for the Pearys and the Amundsens to push to the "uttermost ends." Unlike the man of science, the explorer has completed a definite job: he has unfolded the planet by land and sea. "The last great *earth story*," said Peary, "has been told."

One type of worker in the *new exploration* is the *economist*. Like the man of science, he seeks the causes of outward facts and the laws which govern them. Indeed he is a man of science himself, but of a science whose facts are of such extreme complexity that the laws thus far alleged to govern them consist, for the most part, of a series of contradictory hypotheses. Economists, it would seem, have been unable to agree even upon a definition for their subject. With some (the mercantilists of the eighteenth century) it has been "the science of the possession of precious metals" (but this has been outgrown). With others (the "orthodox economists" and their critics) it amounts to "the science of the production of wealth" under various sets of circumstances. With still others (the utilitarians) it is "the science of the production of welfare or happiness." The names Thomas Mun, Adam Smith, and Jeremy Bentham are the ones commonly associated with these respective schools. Within the Adam Smith and the Bentham schools there are a number of minor schools, some stressing (all unconsciously) the "material fact" of human society, and others the "spiritual form." There are the followers of J. S. Mill and the doctrine of laissez-faire, the definite successors of Adam Smith. Then there are the modifiers and critics of this doctrine, the followers of Karl Marx and of Henry George. There are still others who throw over the laissez-faire doctrine altogether. Thus there would seem to be not one science of economics, but several. But just as one astronomy arose out of the various notions of astrology, so one economics may yet arise out of the present-day fragments. The groping of the economists for a single science must be part and parcel of the process of unraveling the wilderness of human society.

The other type of worker in the new exploration is the *engineer*. The work of the engineer is complemental in a sense to that of the economist: he is a co-worker in the giant task of straightening out the tangle of civilization. But like the doughty explorer of old, he deals with facts—whether actual or potential, rather than with laws—whether confirmed or hypothetic. Not that the engineer is a lawless gentleman. Quite the contrary. He must know the laws—just as Magellan did when he banked on the trade winds to bear him across the "Mar Pacifico." But—like Magellan—he would utilize the laws to convey him to specific destinations. That is what Colonel Goethals did when he visualized the locks in the Panama Canal. That is what is done by the civil engineer who plans a switch-back across the Rocky Mountains. He does not really *plan* the switch-back, he *finds* it—out in the mountains amid the facts and laws of nature. He does not create his own plan, he discovers nature's plan; he reveals a hidden potentiality which nature's laws allow. Likewise with the hydro engineer who harnesses Niagara Falls and develops from a flow of water a flow of electric power. And so with the forest engineer who regulates a region's timber crop and develops therefrom a steady flow of lumber. So also with the agriculturist who develops from a region's farming crops a steady food supply. And with the city planner who controls the flow of a local population. Each one of these is a type of engineer, a man who *finds* rather than *plans* a region's best development: one who builds on the actualities disclosed by exploration. The engineer is the modern explorer.

We have stated that there is more than one "economics." There seems also to be more than one "engineering": we have just mentioned several types—the civil engineer, the hydro engineer, the forest engineer, and others. We have alluded to the possible development some day of a "single economics." Whether or not this ever comes to pass, there are visible evidences of the development, within a future not remote, of a "single engineering."

One illustration of these evidences of the development of a single engineering is provided in the administration of the United States Forest Service, and associated departments, in carrying out the conservation policies initiated two decades ago by the then Chief Forester, Gifford Pinchot, and backed by President Roosevelt. The Forest Service has under its charge the U.S. National Forests, which embrace about 150,000,000 acres of land, the bulk of which lies in the mountainous regions of the far western States. The forest is only one of the natural resources which occur in the National Forest: in addition there are "the soils and the ores and the waters." All four may and do occur inextricably intertwined within a single mountain valley or watershed. Many of these valleys are still undeveloped (or only partly developed), and the problem confronting the Forest Service is the use not alone of the forest resource, but of the others as well. This requires the coördinated visualization of several kinds of specialists or "engineers."

The forest engineer (or "silviculturist") visualizes the use, under a system of forest culture, of the timbered mountain slopes so as to effect a sustained and equable flow of timber from the valley. The agriculturist visualizes the use of the farming areas lying within the bottomlands. The mining engineer may be called in to aid in the development of possible mineral ores within the area. The hydro engineer may be required to visualize the harnessing of the main river or its tributaries for hydro-electric power. The town planner may be required to lay out a prospective permanent lumber town to be located at the entrance of the valley. In addition, the landscape architect may be called in to aid in developing, through a system of trails and cabins and facilities for mountain campers, that further natural resource called "environment." (Through the special efforts of the Forest Service to develop this particular resource, the National Forests are being made to serve the purpose in large measure of the National Parks.) The various plans and visualizations of these specialists must then be integrated in a plan for the whole valley, or region, whereby the highest use is secured from its natural resources as a whole.

A plan of this kind may be called a *regional plan*. It is the product of the "composite mind" of several engineers; it is the product, that is, of a single engineering. Thus we may call it "regional engineering," or by the more usual name of "regional planning."

Another illustration of the development of a single engineering, or of regional engineering, is provided in the project for utilizing the flow of the Colorado River. This river and its tributaries drain a vast territory in the southwestern portion of the country. The flow of these streams affects the welfare of the people living in seven large States, and it may be used, in accordance with local geographic conditions, for three main purposes: for city water supplies; for irrigation; and for hydro-electric power. In addition its utilization and control affect the flooding, or otherwise, of a large area of possible farming land in southern California. A Commission consisting of representatives of the several States affected is working on a comprehensive plan for obtaining the "highest use," for the several purposes mentioned, of this vast and interrelated flow of waters. This project is the first application, on any extensive unit, of the far-visioned policy proposed by the late Senator Francis G. Newlands of Nevada for a national system of river regulation. Senator Newlands embodied his policy in a measure which he presented to Congress in several sessions, but which was never enacted into law.

This Colorado project will involve, and has involved, the construction of storage reservoirs near the headwaters of the various tributary streams, whereby the annual flow of water may be stabilized and excessive flood and low-water stages may be moderated. To prevent these reservoirs from being "silted up" and to equalize further the flow of water running off the steep mountain slopes, special measures of forestry must be practiced thereon to insure a protective forest cover. The operations required in these methods of stream-control, and in the equipment of the streams for the several uses mentioned, necessitate the services of various kinds of engineers. The project requires immediately the civil engineer, the forest engineer, the hydro engineer, and the sanitary engineer. It requires also the agriculturist to estimate the needs of various soils and areas for irrigation, and the industrial engineer to estimate the needs for local mechanical power. And the project, lying as it does at the basis of industrial and regional development generally, requires the statesman himself as engineer to prophesy the needs of future populations. Once more the "composite mind" of a single engineering must be invoked to integrate a galaxy of special advices and schemes and bring forth, again, a *regional plan*.

Let us compare the kind of regional plan illustrated by the Colorado River project with the kind of regional plan illustrated by the National Forest project above cited. In what ways do they differ? The National Forest plan embraces a single tract or locality only—a relatively small contiguous area of perhaps 100,000 acres bounded definitely by the limits of a minor watershed. But the Colorado River plan includes a large number of localities widely separated; it embraces a vast territory covering several States and bounded definitely by the limits of a major watershed. The National Forest plan applies to the geographic aspects of *all* of the main industrial and civic activities within its immediate sphere: lumbering, agriculture, mining, power development, community development, and outdoor recreation. The Colorado River plan applies to the geographic aspects of *one group* only of the activities taking place within its immediate sphere, namely, activities affected by stream flow—city water supply, irrigation, power development, and stream control. The immediate sphere of the National Forest plan consists of, and coincides with, the whole territory embraced within the plan—namely, the tract of 100,000 acres. The immediate sphere of the Colorado River plan consists of certain areas and constructions only within the territory embraced in the plan—namely, the areas irrigated by Colorado waters; the constructions for conducting Colorado waters, and for transmitting power generated therefrom. Roughly speaking, therefore, we may say that the one kind of regional plan affects *all aspects of a single locality*, while the other kind of regional plan affects only *certain related aspects of an indefinitely large territory*.

A third illustration of evidences pointing to the development of a regional engineering is provided in the various projects for altering the structure of the large metropolitan center. Prominent among these projects is the Regional Plan for New York City and Environs. The work done thus far consists of a survey and tentative plan made by the Russell Sage Foundation under the charge of Mr. Thomas Adams. This survey and plan embrace roughly the territory within a radius of fifty miles from Times Square. The immediate sphere of this project consists of the layout, revision, and control of city structures: of streets, bridges, transit lines, and terminal and shipping facilities; of city parks and playgrounds, of business, civic, manufacturing, and residential sections; of the heights and forms of buildings; and of other kindred constructions for aiding the possible functioning of a widening metropolitan area. It is the product of the services of the city planner, the civil and the traffic engineer, and other specialists. The tentative plan is based on the assumption that the area will contain by the year 1950 a population of 29,000,000. It is a painstaking and thorough piece of work; it is certainly a standard, and possibly a finality, with respect to its subject matter. This subject matter is "metropolitan planning" rather than regional planning. It assumes a continually expanding metropolis as an inevitable if not a desirable condition: it views city growth as always taking place along the line of least resistance. This view does not make the distinction—which I shall elaborate in another chapter—between genuinely urban, which furthers an active community life and produces a good environment, and metropolitan growth, which wipes out a good part of community life and produces a deteriorate environment in both town and country.

A fourth illustration pointing toward a regional engineering is provided in the large-scale surveys which have been made in connection with certain strategic industrial projects.

One of these surveys is embodied in the report of the Alaska Railroad Commission made in 1911 in anticipation of the then projected railroad to be built by the United States government to tap the Matanuska coal fields. This report was written by Mr. Alfred H. Brooks of the U.S. Geological Survey, who was a member of the Commission. The railroad then projected, and since built, runs from Seward on the southern coast via the Susitna River valley and the Matanuska region to Fairbanks on the Tanana River, a distance of about 400 miles. A strip of comparatively level alluvial land (potentially agricultural) follows the railroad for most of its length, bounded on both sides by forest-clad slopes whose sharp crestlines form the definite boundaries of a future "industrial watershed" from the Tanana to the sea. The principal resources of this region are soils, forests, coal, and water power. The Commission was instructed by Congress to report on a policy for handling the coal resources only and for lay-

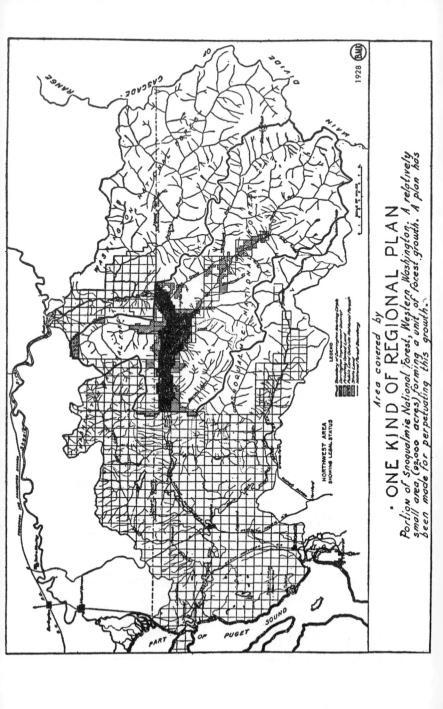

NORTHWEST AREA
SHOWING LEGAL STATUS

LEGEND

· ONE KIND OF REGIONAL PLAN ·

Area covered by

Portion of Snoqualmie National Forest, Western Washington. A relatively small area, (92,000 acres) forming a unit of forest growth. A plan has been made for perpetuating this growth.

1928

Territory covered by
ANOTHER KIND OF REGIONAL PLAN
The Colorado River Basin
A vast area occupying several States and forming a unit of stream flow. A plan is being made for controlling this flow

ing out the railroad and the possible town sites. The policy reported, therefore, consists practically of a regional plan for this Alaska railroad "watershed" corresponding closely with the regional plan above cited for the Colorado River watershed. Each plan embraces an extensive territory, and each plan applies only to certain related activities—those in the one case relating to the flow of water, and in the other case to the flow of coal.

Another one of these surveys is embodied in the report of the International Joint Commission made in 1922 in anticipation of the projected deepening of the canal around the St. Lawrence River rapids. The effect of this deepening would be to make ocean ports of Chicago and the other cities of the Great Lakes, thus diverting commodity flow to the industrial watershed exporting through the St. Lawrence, and away from the overlapping industrial watersheds exporting through New York and the other North Atlantic ports. This little piece of strategy on man's part may be compared with the diversion made by nature herself in past geologic times when the water-flow from the Great Lakes was diverted to its present outlet through the St. Lawrence and away from its former outlet through the Hudson River. Both are natural outlets, and both should be utilized, and so this engineering plan is not so much a scheme of man's as it is part of a basic plan of nature's for "draining" the American continent of its surplus products needed in lands across the seas. The report of the Joint Commission lays no basis for a complete regional plan for distributing wisely the commodity-flow between these two outlets, but it makes a start in that direction; and it indicates a groping, even in competitive times, toward that world-scale "single engineering" which seems destined some day to apply to national and world affairs the same amount of common sense that we now apply to the more readily visualized activities of our everyday personal lives.

A final illustration of regional engineering is provided in the survey embodied in the report of the New York State Housing and Regional Planning Commission, made in 1926. This survey was made in anticipation of no projected railroad or waterway or any other single enterprise. This is how it differs from most of the other large-scale regional projects. It points directly at regional engineering as a normal basis for modern comprehensive living, and not as a series of emergency measures accompanying the "next steps" of industrial expediency. The report was presented to the Governor by Mr. Clarence S. Stein, Commission Chairman, and was written by Mr. Henry Wright.

This report, as stated on its first page, is "not a plan"; it is an analysis of data setting forth the field of planning. The field of planning thus found includes the three needs of cultured man which we have previously stated, namely, the conservation of natural resources, the control of commodity-flow, and the development of environment.

The visualization of the potential workings of these three processes, we must emphasize again, constitutes regional planning, or the complete field to be covered in a regional plan of a given area. This seems likewise to be the Commission's idea of a regional plan: the report stresses the highest use and conservation of the State's natural resources; it points out the fundamental need of controlling commodity-flow, citing the vital flow of dairy products; and finally, in its visualization of "Epoch III," the report pictures, by means of map and text, the development of a possible environment designed for the ultimate objective of "wholesome activity and good living."

In short, the engineering task seen by this New York Commission is the one that has been stated by Governor Alfred E. Smith, namely, "the making of the mold in which future generations shall live." And by "live" the Commission seems to mean a condition of real *living* and not one of mere existence. The Commission seeks to arrive at this end by a control and guidance of present economic forces. Thus the report says:

While the old forces that have shaped the present State are still operating, new forces have come into being to dominate the future. These new forces may be left free to alter the present mold without direction and without control. On the other hand they may be intelligently controlled.

Two of these new forces the report discusses at some length—automobile transport and electric transmission of power. (We might add the radio and the aeroplane.) These forces must, of course, affect profoundly the future movement and distribution of the population. And it is upon the proper distribution of the population (and of the industrial plant whereby the people are supported) that the ultimate solution must depend of the problems we have cited.

Indeed the one problem common to all of the illustrations of regional engineering which we have given is this one of the *flow of population*. And since the population must follow the means of livelihood (the man must follow the job), the basis of population-flow is the *flow of industrial plant*, these two together forming a series of geographic movements (a sort of ebb and flow) of civilization itself. The fundamental problem of regional engineering, therefore, comes down to the control and guidance of industrial migration, and control in such wise as to secure the objectives cited regarding resources, commodities, and environment. In this way may a *single engineering* achieve its application, and attain its final goal—"the making of the mold in which future generations shall live."

What approaches offer themselves in the stupendous task of charting the wilderness of civilization and creating the mold for a genuine culture? Well, they are legion, and a few illustrations have been given from present-day engineering practice. But there seem to be two major approaches to the subject. We have seen from the top of the Times Building two distinct "worlds" to be explored. We may restate them in different terms. They are:

(1) *The metropolitan world:* a framework of world-wide standardized civilization which forms itself around the traffic stream of modern industry and commerce.

(2) *The indigenous world:* a quiltwork of varied cultures, each with its own environment of racial and regional setting—the Chinese, the Hindoo, the Slavic, the British, the American.

One approach of the new exploration is by way of the metropolitan world; the other is by way of the indigenous world.

The metropolitan approach may be made from the top of the highest building of a metropolis. The Times Building will do. The view presents a series of comprehensive questions: From what sources and origins arise the traffic streams converging in the streets below or in the harbor yonder? To what "mouths" or destinations are they

bound? Where are located the natural resources of the
world, and of what do they consist? Where are located
the peoples of the world? Who are these peoples, and what
are their requirements?—in temperate zone, or tropics, or
in humid lands, or arid? At one end of the stream—at the
source or origin—there must be the mine, the farm, the
logging operation; while close by must be the smelter, the
creamery, the sawmill. At the other end of the stream—in
the community of homes which forms the destination—
there must be the store and warehouse whence the people
obtain their finished goods. In between these two extremi-
ties, at various sites along the traffic stream, there stand
the various factories which convert by different stages the
resource into finished product. Where would these roving
factories find their most efficient and strategic resting-
places? Through what line of least resistance, and how
most directly, can resource flow to factory and thence, in
converted form, continue on its way to final warehouse?
We must leave the Times Building for the map of the
world—*outward bound* to explore the terrestrial framework of industrial civilization. It would take a whole book
to show how to get started on this quest; and it must be
another book than this one.

The indigenous approach may be made from the top of
the highest mountain of a region. Both ends of the traffic
stream are present in the view. There are the farms and
forests, and perhaps the open mine pit, from which the
various streams get started. There also is the community
of homes which forms the destination. How can we conserve in fullest measure these soils and forests and ore
lands? How can we develop in fullest measure the inherent environment of home community and landscape?

These are the bottom questions of the indigenous approach. We must leave the mountain and enter the region itself—*inward bound* to explore each community and unit area and chart the highest development of its resource and environment. It will take the remainder of this book to show how to get started on this quest. From now on our exploration will deal with the problems only of the indigenous world, *one of these problems being the invasion thereof by the metropolitan world*. We shall consider only a portion of the "quiltwork" of this indigenous world, namely, the region and culture of eastern or Appalachian America; and shall make our start in the particular region of New England. New England is the most completely settled, the most densely populated, the most historic, and geographically the most varied part of the continent. It holds, in close and concentrated form, every significant problem of regional planning. It is an ideal spot to focus our observations. What can we see from the top of New England?

Chapter IV

SEEN FROM MT. MONADNOCK

What can we see from the top of New England? Where is the top of New England? The highest point is the summit of Mt. Washington. But this is not the point from which to see the largest portion of New England. There is one point, and only one, from which we can look into every New England State, and that is the top of Mt. Monadnock in the southwestern corner of New Hampshire. To any one who has remained long in the northern homeland of America, Mt. Monadnock needs no introduction. It is the Fujiyama of New England. It stands forth in simple solitary majesty, the emblem of a unified homeland, and functions for a natural region as the scepter functions for a royal state. "I have lived in several towns," a housewife said to me once, "but I've always lived in sight of Old Monadnock—so I've always been at home." We have here the lofty pivot of an indigenous region and culture, of a sample pattern of the American quiltwork— a point from which to see "a land" and to contemplate the problems that confront it. What can we *visualize* from this strategic summit?

The view is only *less* bewildering than the view from the top of the Times Building. In lieu of neighboring skyscrapers we see neighboring but more distant mountain ridges; in lieu of deep canyons at our feet we have a dancing sea of hills and dales speckled with field and forest. The horizon of the northwest quadrant consists of the undulating line marked by the Green Mountains of Vermont, a portion of the Great Divide between the Atlantic plain of early English settlement and the interior territory of early French penetration. In the opposite direction, in the southeast quadrant, is visible, with a field glass, not the Times Building but its Boston equivalent, the tower of the Custom House, marking a point on the great line between North America and the Atlantic Ocean. Southward across Massachusetts, between a couple of hills seen in Connecticut and a couple more seen in Rhode Island, lies the gently rolling portion of the New England homeland known as "down country," while northward, backed by the jagged White Mountains, lies the more boisterous and grizzled portion called "up country." Mt. Agamenticus, southern sentinel of the coast of Maine, is seen in the northeast. In the foreground, in all four ways amid the undulations, lies here and there a seat of human habitation—the hill village spotted by the white, shining church spire or the factory town with its black chimney of smoke. Then, all around, a million details—a little section of the world.

Such is what we look at: perhaps also there are white streaming clouds and a tiny thread of smoke called to our attention by the scream of a passing locomotive. We pronounce it all "beautiful," and then—decide that it is time to be going home. But wait! Let us tarry awhile—till we *see* the things we look upon. Let us lay down the field glass and take up a stronger telescope—the eye of the imagination, as we did before from the Times Building. Let us *visualize* once more. From the Times Building we saw two "worlds": there was the metropolitan world all round about us, and there was the indigenous world yonder in the hinterland. What do we see now?

We see the very same two worlds—but from reverse position. On the Times Building (or on its counterpart, the Boston Custom House) we have at our feet the metropolitan world—the "passing streams of traffic" merged in conflux and pouring in from all corners of the land; and we have a glimpse only of the indigenous world—in the distant view of the Hudson Highlands (or of the summit of Mt. Monadnock). But when we go and climb this summit, then we have these "worlds" reversed: then we have at our feet the indigenous world; we have the traffic stream not in conflux or midway, but at its two extremes. We have on one hand the field or forest or resource from which the stream arises, and on the other hand we have the home community to which the stream is destined. But we have in this view a *glimpse* only of the metropolitan world—in the distant view of the factory chimney, the screaming locomotive, or the Boston Custom House.

From now on our exploration will deal with the problems of this indigenous world, one of these problems being, as already stated, the invasion thereof by the metropolitan world. First of all, then, what are the elements of this particular "world" as visualized from the top of Mt. Monadnock?

The indigenous world may be said to be *composed* of natural resources, and these may be divided into three great classes:

(1) Material resources (soils, forests, metallic ores).
(2) Energy resources (the mechanical energy resident in falling water, coal seams, and other natural elements).

(3) Psychologic resources (the human psychologic energy, or happiness, resident in a natural setting or environment).

The term "natural resources," as we have used it in previous chapters, has referred to material resources and mechanical energy alone. These resources have been compared with the geographic element of "land": they form the tangible source of man's existence. The psychologic resources (environment) have been compared with the geographic element of "air." Environment, the contours of the landscape, the arrangement of its vegetation, the visible marks of man's efforts in clearings and fences and farms and gardens and cities as well as in wild forests and mountain areas—environment, in one or all of its many forms, is the pervasive source of man's true living. Raw material and mechanical energy relate to the means of life: environment, whether in natural or in humanized forms, relates to the objectives of life. Man (and civilization), considered as a "material fact," is concerned with the means of life: man (and civilization), considered as a "spiritual form," is concerned with the objectives of life, the pursuit of a higher estate in human development. Raw material and mechanical energy form the terrestrial basis of civilization as a material fact, while environment forms the terrestrial basis of civilization as a spiritual form.

With this distinction in mind, let us make a restatement of the three needs of cultured man, the visualization of which constitutes the new exploration. They are:

The conservation of *physical* natural resources.

The control of commodity-flow.

The development of environment, or *psychologic* natural resources.

We shall in this book deal chiefly with the psychologic natural resources—with the exploration and development of environment. But physical resources and the metropolitan world itself must be included to the extent that they affect the problems of environment. We shall explore, first for the ends, and second for the means: we shall seek first our destination and then the way to get there. In this way we shall emulate the explorers of the past rather than many of the would-be statesmen of the present. We shall take a pattern from Magellan, who first visioned where it was he wished to go, and then discovered how to get there. We shall endeavor to make of this philosophy of regional planning a clean-cut exploration of the destinations of society so far as these can be visualized upon the map. For this reason, we choose, for the subject matter of this book, that particular field of exploration which comes closest to the objectives of life, which is related more to the problems of real living than to those of mere existence. This field is found in the indigenous world and not in the metropolitan; it is found in the world of psychologic natural resources more than in that of physical resources. It is, therefore, the particular world of the *indigenous environment* (and its contacts with other "worlds") that we shall now explore. What manner of environment can we visualize from the top of Mt. Monadnock?

Environment is the product of history—either primal or human history. In order, therefore, to visualize the various types of environment occurring within the horizon of Mt. Monadnock, let us very briefly visualize the history which has taken place therein. This history has been a romantic one—in both its human and primeval aspects. Roughly speaking, its main dramatic events have consisted of three great "invasions" to which the region has been subjected.

The first invasion was that of the great *ice-flow*. This came out of the north. It was more than a hundred centuries ago. It drubbed the country more fiercely than could a thousand modern armies. The ancient life of that time—of forest, beast, and bird—was ruthlessly shoved aside. The rocky summits of the mountain ranges were rubbed down and subdued as by a huge piece of sandpaper in the hands of some terrestrial giant. Below in the lowlands the rivers themselves were driven from their courses; lakes were molded; hills were made—and unmade. Thus all of New England was finally submerged, and the Arctic ice cap fronted on what we now call Long Island Sound. And then, in its own good time, and with frigid dignity, it retreated and went back into the north . . . Life started over again—on Mt. Monadnock and all around. New forests came, and beasts and birds. It was like the Creation come once more; and gradually through the millennia the modern forest primeval was brought to pass. To the new "civilizations" of bird and beast was added that of aboriginal man. And thus it went for over a hundred centuries in what is now New England.

Meantime some humanly significant things were beginning to happen. After fifty centuries or more, some Pyramids were built in Egypt; then, after another thirty centuries, the Christian era dawned. Then time was being measured and dates recorded. But not on Mt. Monadnock. The year 1066 came along, and England was invaded by the Conqueror. Then came 1492: still the mountain top slept on. Then 1620. If Old Monadnock and her sister mountains could have had feelings, they might now have felt a little nervous. For Plymouth Rock in 1620 formed the base of a second great invasion.

This was a flow—not of ice, but of *population*. European civilization was on the rampage. It was pushing westward. Out of the east this time came another inevitable flow. It acted like the first, though far less thoroughly. Again the forests were felled and the landscape remolded. But fields and villages came instead of ice-sheets. There came Dublin and Fitzwilliam and Jaffrey and many another colonial village. The landscape, once primeval, now turned colonial. A new environment came over it and clothed it. As primeval America grew up after the great ice-flow of the distant past, so indigenous human America grew up after the great folk-flow of 1620. But the mountain ranges held their grizzled forest clothing high above the colonial invasion, and here for one place primeval America lived on.

Primeval New England since the glacial age was developing during upward of a hundred centuries; colonial New England was developing during about two centuries. Then came a *third invasion*. It came as another inroad of civilization. It started from Boston in the 1830's. It started with the railway and the steam engine. Later it took on electricity and gasoline. The result was the growth of the metropolis which we have described: not alone the big metropolis but the little imitation, a species of standardized excrescence which has tended to replace the original colonial city. The influx of this excrescence follows the grooves set by the railway and the motor road as accurately as the ancient ice-sheet followed the grooves set by the open valleys. Its influence, popping up along these grooves—in Socony station, in chain store, in the hot-dog stand, and in Main Street generally—compares with the tentings of an incoming army. This influx we may call the third, or *metropolitan invasion*.

The result of these three invasions consists in three distinct environments—the primeval, the colonial, and the metropolitan. The first two constitute in New England and America what amounts to the "indigenous world"— the primal and the human halves. *The contact of the indigenous with the metropolitan world* forms the basic problem of regional planning, and one of the big problems of modern civilization: it will form, therefore, the main theme of the following chapters in this Philosophy of Regional Planning.

Chapter V

THE INDIGENOUS AND THE METROPOLITAN

We have had a view from the top of New England. We have sighted our main theme—the contact of the indigenous and the metropolitan: two "worlds," two ideas of life, as distinct perhaps as the Greek and the Roman, and yet interwoven in utmost intimacy. The first job of our exploration will be to visualize their separate strands. Each is a separate environment: the indigenous appears to be a compound of the primeval and the colonial; the metropolitan appears to be a compound of the urban and the world-wide industrial. But let us watch appearances. In order to understand these compound environments better, and to separate their strands more readily, we shall analyze them into their various elements. There seem to be three basic "elemental environments," as we might call them. They are the following:

The Primeval—the environment of life's sources, of the common living-ground of all mankind.

The Rural—the environment of agriculture, of local common interests and all-round human living.

The Urban—the environment of manufacturing and trade, of the community of group interests and specialized living.

Let us look into each one of these:

The Primeval Environment. Abraham Lincoln once had this to say about Niagara Falls:

The mere physical of Niagara Falls is a very small part of that world's wonder. Its power to excite reflection and emotion is its great charm. . . . It calls up the indefinite past. When Columbus first sought this continent—when Christ suffered on the cross—when Moses led Israel through the Red Sea—nay, even when Adam first came from the hand of his Maker: then, as now, Niagara was roaring here.

Thus spoke "the first American" about primeval America. This picture of the "mere physical" of America, and of "its power to excite reflection," makes a rough and ready visualization of the particular type of primeval environment on which the American nation was founded. Here is America of the "indefinite past," the America which "was roaring here" when "Columbus first sought this continent." Of course every other nation also has been founded ultimately upon some primeval base. But we are close to ours. Primeval America is well within the memory of men now living, and in spots it still hangs on. Such names as Daniel Boone and Lewis and Clark set forth a clean-cut background of mountain, forest, plain, and Indian life, whose yet unfaded color lingers on a people's retina and holds alive such other names as Niagara and Monadnock and Appalachian.

We spell these names and place them on our maps. We cleave to them as symbols anyhow of the happy hunting-ground for which they stood. We visualize the *name*. Our job now, in the new exploration, is to visualize the *thing*— the hunting-ground itself as a land in which to live, the actual restoration of the primeval American environment. In this we must take one region at a time. We are taking New England. Here indeed the true primeval has been largely swept away, though the spruce and fir of the Northwoods preserve much of their wild flavor (in Aroostook, in Coos, in the White and Green Mountains, and elsewhere). But the remote lands of New England, if not wholly primeval, are in large part *pastoral*. The semi-wooded upland pastures on the slopes and rugged summits of "up country" form an approach at least to the primeval, and give us definite sense of our "indefinite past."

Other types of the primeval American environment occur in other parts of America: the luxuriant hardwood forests of the Carolina Highland; the semi-tropical swamps of the Gulf Coast; the Arizona desert; the fir-flanked Cascades. Here in this "happy hunting-ground" we find the sources of life itself—in the forests, the waters, and the rest of nature's gifts. Here is our common *living-ground*.

The Rural Environment. As with the primeval environment, so with the rural—various American types have existed. These have been developed under various racial and climatic combinations: the Puritans in New England; the Cavaliers in Virginia; the French in Quebec and in Louisiana; the Spanish in California; the Scandinavian in Minnesota. The primeval environment is one bequeathed to us by God. All others are bequeathed by God with man's assistance. Hence enters, with man, the element of fallacy. But some environments approach more closely the primal needs than do some others: they reflect the wants of man *as* man (as genus Homo) rather than man as any particular race. One of these seems to be the environment brought over and developed by the Puritans in New England during our pre-Revolutionary period (1620 to 1776). To this we have already referred as the "colonial environment."

This is a type of rural environment; it is illustrated in

the New England hill village. Though developed in its present form within recent centuries, it has come down to us from early Anglo-Saxon days; and its essential roots extend, probably, back into unrecorded times. The hill village is a pronounced example of a unit of humanity—a community—a definite "living together." The essence of its being is reflected in its physical layout. The Common is the nucleus of the village life—physically, legally, socially, for in and around this are fitted the various elements of human activity in all the structural symmetry of a starfish.

There are about five points to this starfish: religion, politics, education, commerce, home. There is the church (with its steeple); there is the town hall (with its stately Doric columns); and the little red brick school house; and the general store; and the thirty or so dwelling-houses, these last being placed around the Common and along the radiating roads. Tributary to this nucleus lies the territory within, say, a three-mile radius, which, with its fields of corn and hay, its sheep and cattle pastures, and its woodlots of white pine and hardwoods, forms (or once did form) the "physical resource" whose workings provide (or did once provide) the employment and support of the men and families constituting the little unit. And then, as part of the workings, there stood, along the stream at the bottom of the hill (in the real old colonial days), the three infant manufactures of food, clothing, and shelter, represented in the grist mill, shoddy mill, and sawmill.

The structural symmetry of the colonial environment was equaled by its cultural symmetry. The rural colonial village embodied a rounded, if elementary, development of genuine culture—physical, intellectual, artistic. Each season, being a reality and not a weather report, had its suitable activity. The "all-roundness" of colonial community living may be illustrated by noting some of its old-time play activities, showing as they do a primal, natural balance between outdoors and indoors, daytime and night, summer and winter.

There was the swimming-hole in the mill stream—and the flooding of the meadow for skating around the evening bonfire. There was the "after haying" picnic on the river intervale—and the "double-runner" coasting parties by February moonlight. There was baseball—and there was shinny: rainy-day pout fishing—and tracking rabbits. There was the mud scow on the spring meadow—and there was fishing through the ice. There was the illustrated lecture—on the planetary bodies or the Norman Conquest. There was *Evangeline* read aloud on a long solstice evening. There were May baskets on twilight doorsteps, with loud knockings and merry routs for conquest; there was "drop the handkerchief" on the Common. There was the midsummer authors' carnival. There was the strawberry festival on the green and the corn-husking on the barn floor. There was the farmers' supper and the ladies' autumn fair. (There were quadrilles and reels and slides.) There was the Grand Masquerade in the January thaw. The church bell rang out on the night before the Fourth, as the sleigh bells did on the night before Christmas.

This array of colonial cultural activity is not given in order to picture an ideal. Nor is it a dream of village life in eighteenth-century New England. In every one—and more—of the customs cited, I have myself taken part personally since the 1880's. Colonial village culture, therefore, is still near at hand. Of English origin, it is indigenous specially to New England, for here it developed its American form. Here still lie its deeply imbedded roots. The atmosphere of the colonial village and the mists arising from the primeval Niagara, both are imbedded in the indigenous America, both come to us out of "the indefinite past."

The Urban Environment. Frederic C. Howe has written an illuminating book called *The City: The Hope of Democracy.* Personally I am in thorough agreement with this hope—that is, for the *real city.* And if the real city is the hope of democracy, and self-government, then it seems to be the hope of something far deeper; namely, the ability of human kind happily to live together. As the ant hill or the beehive is a highly organized and concentrated community of the insect world, so the city is with respect to the human world. The city is a community *par excellence.* It is the village grown up—with the several points of the starfish symmetry developed to their fullest measure. But, understand—there is the same difference between the grown-up village and the overgrown village as between the grown-up youth and the overgrown boob. Village and city—each is *a community*—each is (or should be) for a population what the home should be for a family.

Let us look into our complete, symmetrical city, as a ready method of getting at the essence of the real urban environment. Our city is not only urban, but urbane; not merely the material fact, but also the spiritual form; not industrial alone, but cultural as well. Each point in our starfish is developed to a measure limited only by the confines of our civilization. The meeting-house becomes a cathedral; the town hall becomes the City Hall or the

dome-topped legislative Capitol; the little red school becomes a humming university, and the store, a whirling
terminal. The home remains a home. But inter-home relations must seek a different basis, since you have too many
neighbors now to have *all* of them as intimates. A vital
common interest in the Common will remain (provided
the city is a real community), but the intimacy of friendship must be limited to numbers it can comprehend.
Groups, therefore, are inevitable and new bonds of comradeship; and these are based less on geographic interest
in any particular city section than on zeal for some section of the world or civilization. There is the "section" of
sport, of art, of music, of drama, of literature, of science,
of religion, of statesmanship, of technology, of economics,
of what not. Thus are the points on the starfish subdivided
and developed, each one, toward the nth power of our
dreamed-for realization.

Each one of these groups is a little sphere unto itself.
The city is not only a community, it is a conflux. We have
already emphasized the point that the metropolis is a
conflux of streams of traffic. So is the city. The real city,
as a center of industry, is a conflux of streams of traffic; as
a center of culture it is a conflux of streams of thought.
Indeed each group is such a conflux. The single group
within a city is like the post office in that city. The posted
letter is a drop of water in a stream of ideas. Each such
drop of water, starting in some home or business office or
other source, flows first to the central postal station, thence
to the station of some remote or near-by center, and thence
again to some other home or business office, or some other
destination. In each city post office certain streams converge, while others radiate outward. So with each group

of people within that city who are occupied in the development of a single body of ideas—whether of business, or politics, or religion, or science, or art. Each group is a "station," having definite connections with many other stations; and around each, wherever it may be, there converge and radiate a myriad streams of thought. In this way each group within a city may form part of a world-wide whole, and to the extent to which this is so, we call such city in the true sense *cosmopolitan*.

Cosmopolitan does not mean standardized. Quite the reverse. It means adding to the world's variety rather than detracting therefrom. To borrow foreign ideas which can be adapted to our local or regional environment is one thing; to inflict our own patterns on foreign lands, regardless of their environments, is quite another thing. For us to borrow china tableware from the Chinese or skis from the Norwegians, or for the Indian to borrow the riding-horse from the European, who had got it from the Asiatic— these are cosmopolitan adaptations to home environment which enrich the color of the world by translating beauty from one country's medium into another's. For us to perpetrate upon the various peoples of the earth, regardless of race, land, or climate, a standard pattern of American pantaloons, or American cigars, or American movies— these are metropolitan intrusions on home environment which pauperize the color of the world by transporting ugliness from the factories of one country to the living-quarters of all others. Cosmopolitanism adds to the world's variety: metropolitanism adds to the world's monotony.

The city which is truly cosmopolitan is also individual, while the standardized city may be crudely provincial. An instance of the first is the City of Quebec: she is (or was when I first saw her) a capital instance of a city with a personality. She is French, and she is English; her reposeful heights reflect the Arctic wilderness and the early Canadian frontier, while her Lower Town suggests the Middle Ages: because she has variety, she is individual. On the other hand, take any of a dozen American so-called cities: if you have seen one, you have seen all; they have geometry, not personality.

A city, to be an individual, must first of all have unity: to be an interesting individual, it must to some extent be cosmopolitan. These seem to be the two bedrock essentials of the true urban environment. The unity must be of body and of soul. There must be definite geographic boundaries as with the early New England village, and no petering out in fattening, gelatinous suburban fringes: the true city is all heart with no fatty degeneration. There must be a common interest and soul—something equivalent to the village Common. Such combined unity, of form and substance, makes the complete community. The real city is the complement of the real village. One is a community of groups and specialized interests; the other is a community of human folks and all-round interests. In the one are focused world-wide forces through the medium of specialized cosmopolitan contacts; in the other, nearer alike to earth and to sky, are focused world-deep and cosmic forces through the more intimate medium of human and primal contacts.

We have now looked into each of the three basic elemental environments, the primeval, the rural, and the urban. We have viewed each as a normal entity. Let us next look into them as they actually occur as a part of present American life: view them, that is, as actual and somewhat abnormal entities. We shall take them up in reverse order, beginning with the urban environment. This environment in America has been so transformed that it may be considered as practically extinct, and the process itself of transformation may best be described by using an analogy and comparing the city to a pond.

As a city is defined as a "large town," so a lake may be defined as a "large pond." Suppose we have a little mill-pond, made by damming up a creek where it flows through a canyon. Say we want to enlarge our pond; that is, turn it into *a lake*. We build a higher dam, closing the canyon to a higher level. The waters of the creek and mill-pond rise to this higher level throughout the upper valley, deepening the mill-pond and widening its surface both upstream and on the sides. The pond becomes a lake.

Suppose this lake to be as large as can be held within the confines of the valley. It is bounded securely by crest-lines on each side. But in one of these crestlines there is a gap, the bottom of which comes down within a few feet of the lake's surface.

Well, it is suggested that we have a larger lake: that we have a *super-lake*. So we raise the dam still higher. The waters begin to rise and extend their boundaries. They reach the level of the bottom of the gap. Still they go on rising. They begin to spill over the gap into the adjoining valley. Still the waters rise. They begin to flood the adjoining valley. Pretty soon they form a deluge.

Our lake, which was intact within its natural proper sphere (the valley), has now become a ruptured thing and uncontrolled. It spreads itself in headless devastating flight, knowing no confines. A "super-lake" indeed!

Of course no civil engineer would be idiot enough ever to let this happen; ever to allow the flow of the waters to get outside their safe and proper sphere. But we the people of this country, and of the world in general, allow this very thing to happen. Not with the flow of waters—no, but with the flow of population.

Not content in making a small town into a large town; in developing merely a larger community—a unit of humanity within its natural borders and confines: not content in making a *city*, we make a *super-city*. We handle the advancing flow of population toward the urban centers just as a mentally deficient engineer would handle the advancing flow of water down the valley. First we build a "dam." This consists of office buildings where jobs are to be had. The population must reach these office buildings in order to make a living. Then we allow the flood of folks to back up against this "dam" of office buildings until it backs far outside the confines of an integrated city and spills over on adjoining areas. This it does in a shapeless widening deluge of headless suburban massings which know no bounds or social structure.

What we call "suburban" (the under-city) is really "super-urban" (the over-city—the outer layers of the tide which overwhelms the city). Since there is usually no sharp line between suburbs and city proper, we have, in such centers as New York, Chicago, Detroit, and the other "Greater" cities, in truth no *city* at all. Instead we have what Mr. W. J. Wilgus of the New York Central Lines has graphically called a "massing of humanity."

These massings and floods of humanity follow closely

the law which governs the massings and floods of waters—the law of gravitation. In level country, like the prairie around Chicago, they just spread out in an ever-widening disk. In hill country they creep through the valleys or along the shore lines, coalescing in linear bands, as up the Hudson valley or along the shore between Bridgeport and New Haven. They submerge whatever stands in their advancing path, whether village or open country. Thus the "hill village" retains its integrity as a community only so long as the tide remains below, but too often it has, like its sister village in the valley, been overpowered by the creeping mass and drowned beneath its waters. And so Arlington Heights and Lexington within the Boston Basin, as Harlem and Chelsea long since upon Manhattan Island, have taken their places among the submerged villages of America.

But the first thing to become submerged is not the country village but the city itself as a true community. Since, as already noted, there is no clear-cut line between the city and the suburban (or super-urban) fringes, the city precincts become swallowed in the "lake" as much as the surrounding areas, and whatever color there may be in the original *urban environment* "runs" in the watery colorless fringes and becomes diluted into the all-pervading and standardized drabness of the *metropolitan environment*. That is what has happened to "Boston Town" and to "Little Old New York." It has happened to Washington, D. C., within my own memory, and it has happened to a dozen other American centers. These now have become "Great Cities" and hope to become "Titan Cities." Mr. Clarence S. Stein has a better name for them: he calls them "Dinosaur Cities." In each case the adjective is correct, but the substantive is nil; for, having ceased to be communities, they are no longer *cities*. Indeed *the city is the first victim of the metropolitan flood*.

And this situation is not to be dodged merely by having middle-sized towns. We have them now in plenty: so many in fact that we have a name for them—we call them "Main Streets." The average "Main Street" is neither village nor city. If it is yet a community it hopes soon not to be: it dreams to become, not a social structure like ancient Athens, but a social gelatin like modern New York. It is not a unit of humanity, it is an incipient "massing of humanity." It is, if anything, worse than the "Great City" itself. Cosmopolitan interests and contacts tend to mellow the metropolitanism of the one, while crass provincialism rowdyizes the metropolitanism of the other.

The true urban environment, therefore, seems to be submerged in America, for the time being, at all events, by what we have called the metropolitan environment. The city is being supplanted by the super-city. The community of definite social structure, developing within certain geographic confines around a common civic purpose, is being replaced by a standardized massing of humanity void of social structure, unbound by geographic confines, and uninspired by any common interest. Intimate self-government is being ironed out by generalized overhead administration. Mechanical standardization replaces human integration. Such seems to be the present actual situation respecting the urban environment. How about the rural environment?

The rural environment in America has also undergone a transformation, especially in the older portions of the country. The colonial village which we have pictured has, as an actuality, very largely disappeared. It has gone in two ways. First it has been submerged, in the manner already described, by the metropolitan "waters" of the super-city. This has been the fate of the villages lying within the great metropolitan districts—Boston, New York, and the other districts in eastern or Appalachian America. Next it has been "drained" to augment the "waters." This has been the fate largely of the villages lying within the back hill country of the Appalachian barrier itself. The disappearance in these two ways of the country village is reflected in the statistics of rural population of Appalachian America (the Atlantic and east central States). This in 1800 formed 96 per cent. of the total population; that is, almost everybody in America was then living in settlements containing less than 2,500 persons each. In 1920 only 43 per cent. of the people in this portion of America were living in rural settlements or areas. In New England the proportion has shrunk to 21 per cent.

The typical colonial village which we have described has become, in the up country of New England, for the most part a deserted village. The church and steeple remain, and the bell also, but it rings, if it rings at all, for a season only, and then for a waning congregation. The town hall is there, but the town meeting has been moved to a more populous precinct. The school house stands, but the pupils who are left in town are "merged" by motor bus in some other center. The independent store has become a chain store. The thirty dwelling-houses have become thirteen—or three. The outlying fields and pastures have largely become brushland (having shrunk since 1890 by

43 per cent.), and the woodlots are cut off a little faster than they grow. Below in the valley the grist mill has gone; the shoddy mill went long ago; the sawmill run by water power has been replaced by the steam portable.

The primeval environment, like the rural, has been affected in two ways. It has not been submerged, but vital particles of it have been captured by the influence of metropolitanism and made to some extent a portion of the metropolitan environment itself. This happens when a lofty summit like Mt. Washington, the acme of a little primeval world, is profaned and half obliterated by the erection of a modern hotel connected by cog-rail and motor road with the tourist world below. The complete primeval environment on a site of this kind consists of two halves: first, the summit itself as the superlative sample of the realm; and second, the vision in perspective of the realm in its entirety. The hotel leaves us the second half, impaired somewhat by the cacophony of the immediate environs; it practically obliterates the first half.

The other outstanding way in which the primeval environment has been affected is by depletion of the forests. This point has long been emphasized, and by many able writers and exponents. The development of the forest as a psychologic resource must go hand in hand with the development of timber as a physical resource, and this will come to pass when, gradually, timber mining is replaced by timber culture.

We have now examined, both as normal potentialities and as present actualities, the three "elemental environments." Together they seem to form, when normally developed, a complete and rounded external world adapted to man's psychologic needs. The primeval is the environment of man's contact with nature; the rural (or communal) is the environment of fundamental human relations; the urban (or cosmopolitan) is the communal environment compounded. Each one of these spheres is a basic natural resource in man's development, and depletion in any one of them means a corresponding depletion in man's life.

Each of these environments is rooted squarely in the earth, not only the primeval and the communal but the cosmopolitan as well, for this is merely a collection of indigenous experiences from other lands. They form the indigenous world, the fundamental world of man's needs as a cultured being. In a sense they form the substance of the ideal world of normal contacts and reactions wherein the course of man's evolution might run smoothly were it not for the injection therein from time to time of some exotic substance. Something of this sort seemingly has come to pass, in America and elsewhere, within the past century. A rootless, aimless, profoundly disharmonized environment has replaced the indigenous one.

This new world is the metropolitan world. It is "a world without a country." Its reactions are born not of nature's soil, but of artificiality; they are reverse to the reactions of the natural normal sphere. Instead of means being adapted to achieve ends, the ends are distorted to fit established means; in lieu of industry being made to achieve culture, culture is made to echo the intonations of industry; oil paints are manufactured not to promote art, art is manufactured to advertise oil paints. Yet this unnatural tendency of the metropolitan process has come about in a seemingly natural way. The machine spells freedom from primitive industry and raw-boned nature, and if one machine makes one unit of freedom, then, we argue, ten machines must make ten units. But, of course, they do no such thing. We wake up to find ourselves no longer serfs to nature's soil but to find ourselves instead the slaves to man's machine. We have within our exogenous world swapped the old boss for a new one. The mastership belongs no longer to nature in the raw, but to "nature dressed up in modern clothes."

The great struggle of the immediate future will be between man himself and man's machine. One form of this struggle promises to be a contest between two realms. One of these is that potential realm of permanent human innate desire, whose power awaits its development to actuality even as the potential sphere of water power within the mountain stream. This human realm (or sphere) has in America a twofold residence: first in the gradually awakening common mind of a large portion of the country's people; and second in the actual territory and landscape of a large portion of the country itself. This potential awakening common mind, groping unconsciously for a complete environment, would base itself on psychologic resource as well as physical, and, to secure man's innate natural ends, would harness *the machine* as the machine has harnessed natural means and power. This we may call the innate or indigenous portion of civilization. The other realm consists of the exogenous or metropolitan portion. Here is the real war of civilization.

This struggle will be taking place not alone in America, but on every other continent. It will be a contest between the aggressive mechanized portion of Western European society (so-called Western civilization) and the indigenous portion of every society invaded, including the indigenous portion of American society. The contest in this country will be between Metropolitan America and Indigenous America. These now stand vis-à-vis, not only psychologically but physically and geographically. The metropolitan world we have compared to a mechanized framework; also we have compared it to an invading army and to an invading flood of water. It is all of these: it is a mechanized molten framework of industry which flows, as we have said, in accordance with the law of gravitation. First it occupies the lower valley, such as the locality of the Boston Basin, obliterating the original urban environment of "Boston Town." Next in finger-like projections it flows, glacier-wise, toward the outskirts, obliterating such rural village and environment as comes within its wake. Then, its projections narrowing, it flows along the railways and motor roads back through the hinterland, starting little centers of provincial metropolitanism in the Main Street towns and around the numerous gasoline stations. Finally here and there it crawls up some mountain summit and obliterates a strategic particle of the primeval environment. It is mightiest in the valleys and weakest on the mountain ridges. The strategy of the indigenous world is just the other way. It is still mighty within the primeval environment, as along the ridgeways of the Appalachian barrier, including such ranges as the Green Mountains in New England. It is strong also in such regions as up country, where, although the farms and villages are depleted, the resources both physical and psychologic are still there, and are yet open to restoration and renewed development. But down in the lower valleys and around the big centers the metropolitan world, as we have shown, is in virtual possession, and any improvement in environment awaits the complex process of reformation from within.

The metropolitan world, then, may be considered as an exotic intrusion or "flow" into certain portions of the innate or indigenous world. Considered thus, and not merely as a static framework, it becomes the dominant part of the flow of population and of the industrial migration to which we have referred in a previous chapter. The control and guidance of this flow and migration we have stated to be the fundamental problem of regional engineering toward the goal set up by Governor Smith of New York, which was "the making of the mold in which future generations shall live." The particular aspect of this problem treated of in this Philosophy of Regional Planning is the strategy of the indigenous world with respect to its contact with this metropolitan flow. This strategy consists, roughly speaking, in developing the indigenous environments (primeval, rural, and communal) and in confining the encroachments of the metropolitan environment. As applied to this country, therefore, it consists in developing the Indigenous America and in confining the Metropolitan America. This procedure requires the consideration of a number of important questions with respect both to ends and to means, as well as to further background on the subject of the American setting. We shall, therefore, look next into something of the history and causes which have shaped the particular contact in this country of indigenous and metropolitan environments as these have been disclosed in the present chapter.

Chapter VI

AMERICAN MIGRATIONS

In a period of flow, men have the opportunity to remold themselves and their institutions.

Lewis Mumford in these words opens one of his illuminating articles [1] in the field of regionalism. He goes on to point out that we in America are now in a period of flow and hence in a period of opportunity. The particular problem before us concerns the remolding of the Metropolitan America in its contact with the Indigenous America. The Metropolitan America, as we have seen, is at present in a condition of flow. This condition is the result of certain previous flows, or migrations, of the American population. These migrations, therefore, are potent causes in shaping the particular contact in this country between indigenous and metropolitan environments. Let us look into these American migrations.

Historically, according to Mumford, there are "two Americas: the America of the settlement and the America of the migrations." He defines them both:

The first America consists of the communities that were planted on the seaboard and up the river valleys during the seventeenth and eighteenth centuries. By 1850 these communities had achieved their maximum development; they had worked out a well-rounded industrial and agricultural life, based upon the fullest use of their regional resources through

[1] "The Fourth Migration," by Lewis Mumford. *Survey Graphic*, May, 1925 (Regional Planning Number).

the water-wheel, mill, and farm, and they had created that fine provincial culture, humbly represented in the schools, universities, lyceums, and churches, which came to a full efflorescence in the scholarship of Motley, Prescott, Parkman, and Marsh, and in the literature of Emerson, Thoreau, Melville, Whitman, and Poe.

What I have defined as the *Indigenous America* is this "America of the settlement" plus such influence thereof as went west over the Allegheny Mountains. Speaking in terms of statesmanship and personality, it is the America of Washington and Jefferson and Franklin.

The second America is the America of the migrations; the first migration that cleared the land west of the Alleghenies and opened the continent, the work of the land pioneer; the second migration, that worked over this fabric a new pattern of factories, railroads, and dingy industrial towns, the bequest of the industrial pioneer; and finally . . . the third migration, the flow of men and materials into our financial centers, the cities where buildings and profits leap upward in riotous pyramids. These three migrations have covered the continent and knitted together its present framework.

What I have defined as the *Metropolitan America* is this "America of the migrations"—the America resulting in the present metropolitan framework. This framework, the product of three migrations, is itself in a state of flow, and its movement constitutes the fourth migration, or "metropolitan invasion." * Speaking again in terms of personality, it is the America of George F. Babbitt, the realtor of Zenith and Floral Heights.

Let us look a little more closely at each of these four

* The fourth migration is the *present phase* of the metropolitan invasion.

migrations. The first migration was an outgoing trans-continental movement led by the covered wagon. Its slogan was "Westward Ho!" This movement or "flow," like most population-flows, was directed toward a source of livelihood. The source in this case consisted of the free lands of the public domain in the West. Except for Kentucky, Tennessee, and Texas, all territory west of the original thirteen States has been owned outright by the United States government, which has turned much land over to the settler (in farm units usually of 160 acres), either for the asking or for a nominal sum. The same year (1776) which began American political independence likewise began American expansion as a continental nation, for in that year Daniel Boone first crossed the Appalachian mountain barrier and started the frontier on its great western journey. Three-quarters of a century later, with the gold rush of '49, a counter frontier was projected eastward from the Pacific Coast when the front of the western movement had reached lower Wisconsin, Kansas City, and eastern Texas. These approaching frontiers in the 1880's met and mingled in the wide intervals among the Rocky Mountains, and the bulk of America's wilderness became thereby a settled land. Thus took place in the course of one century the establishing, from coast to coast, of the agricultural industry and the American farmer. This first flow of the American population is readily visualized upon the map, forming as it did a tangible, broad-gauged continental *outflow*.

The second migration was a remolding transcontinental movement led by the "iron horse." The seed of this movement was the union of two mechanical inventions—the steam engine and the tramway. This union was first made

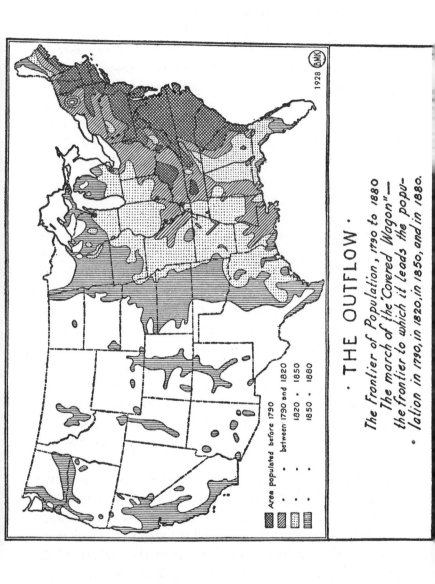

· THE OUTFLOW ·

The Frontier of Population, 1790 to 1880
The march of the "Covered Wagon"—
the frontier to which it leads, the popu-
· lation in 1790, in 1820, in 1850, and in 1880.

	Area populated before 1790
	, between 1790 and 1820
	, , , 1820 - 1850
	, , , 1850 - 1880

1928 BMK

in England by Stephenson in 1829 when "The Rocket" made its first successful trip. It took one short year for this seed to reach America, where in 1830 there were 23 miles of railway put in use, this mileage consisting of the first link of the B. & O. out of Baltimore and of the line started from Albany to Schenectády. During 50 odd years before this, the covered wagon had been carrying westward the frontier of population until now it rested just beyond the Mississippi River. So the iron horse in 1830 started after the covered wagon and soon caught up with it. In 1854, with the frontier advanced to the Missouri River, continuous railway service had reached the Mississippi; in 1869, with the frontier lingering in Nebraska, the first Pacific Railway had shot through to the Golden Gate. By 1890 the bulk of the American railway network was completed, including four lines to the Pacific Coast. Thus in a little more than half a century the first great railway empire was established, and with it a second spreading of the population.

But this second migration led to something more than a railway empire; it led to an empire of steam. The source of livelihood which now was sought consisted partly of free land and the farm, but more and more it came to be employment in the factory and shop. Especially was this true in and among the big coal and iron sections of the northeast quarter of the country, where the railway net became the thickest. As the covered wagon led a population to the farm, so the iron horse led another population to the factory. The iron horse led the way to the iron man: it led to the machine—the machine in the factory of the small, dingy, smoky manufacturing town. The first flow (or outflow) of the American population placed on the face of the continent the first pioneer civilization—that of the agricultural industry and the American farmer; the second flow (or reflow) of the population remolded and augmented this pioneer civilization by establishing the grimy manufacturing industry and the American factory worker. The first migration may be visualized as an outflow, the second as a *reflow*.

The third migration consisted (and consists) of a series of local in-drawing movements attracted by the city skyscraper. The farm in this case has been forsaken as a means of livelihood. The source of employment herein sought dwells partly in the factory and in the industry of producing goods, but more and more is it coming to dwell in the office building and in the business of selling goods. This business has many ramifications. For the most part it exists on paper. The tangible product of agriculture is evidenced in pounds of food and raw textile; that of manufacturing, in the objects of a great variety of products and by-products; the tangible result of salesmanship is manifested in bushels of letter files and of printed literature. The office building is a word-factory. Its words relate to financial dealings, to property records, to legal snarls and convolutions, to advertising exhortations, to newspaper harangues, and to other hectic matters of "overhead" supervision and of general "go-getting." Such machinations require a host of men and of young ladies to lay down the law and ply the typewriter, and a host of store clerks to keep them fed and clothed in garments appropriately dapper to their paper calling. Still another host of workers is required to carry all these people (as already noted) from "places where they would rather not live to places where they would rather not work, and back again." More

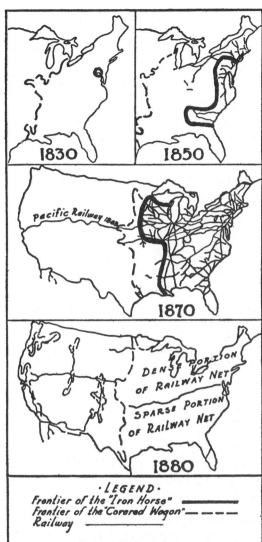

1830

1850

Pacific Railway 1869

1870

DENSE PORTION
OF RAILWAY NET

SPARSE PORTION
OF RAILWAY NET

1880

· LEGEND ·
Frontier of the "Iron Horse" ———————
Frontier of the "Covered Wagon" ——— ——— ———
Railway ———————

· THE REFLOW ·

The Frontier of Railway Growth, 1830 to 1880
The "Iron Horse" races the "Covered Wagon"
The frontiers of each are shown in 1830, in 1850,
in 1870, and in 1880.

1928

hosts are needed to build the skyscrapers, the stores, the subways, and the suburban so-called "homes." But the "industry on paper" just described is the cause of all the rest.

This paper industry of "overhead" is the *cause* and foundation of the strictly metropolitan industries, as the factory was of the strictly urban or small-town industries. But it is the *effect* of the continental industries—those of agriculture, lumbering, mining, manufacturing, transportation, and the others which operate throughout the continent. It seems indeed to consist of a crude attempt at the integrated management or direction of these continental industries. The rise in America of this "overhead industry" dates from the period of the big industrial consolidations which got under way in the 1880's. This was the time, as we have seen, when the country's settlement was practically completed with the merging of the frontiers in the far western States, and when the railway net had nearly covered its ultimate territory. Since that time the "overhead industry" has increased with leaps and bounds, followed by the development of the metropolitan massings which we have previously described.

What I have called the "overhead industry" and the "industry on paper," Mr. Lewis Mumford calls by the more dignified term of "financial direction." He sums up concisely its relation to the third migration:

The magnet of the third migration was the financial center. As the industrial system developed in America productive effort came to take second place to financial direction, and in the great consolidations of industry that began in the 'eighties, in the growth of banking and insurance facilities in the 'nineties, and in the development of advertising for the purpose of securing a national market, that got under way in the present century, the sales and promotion departments have absorbed, directly or indirectly, a large part of the population.

I shall adopt Mr. Mumford's term "financial direction," and shall include within its meaning not only the control and promotion of financial affairs purely, but of matters concerning property, legality, advertising, publicity, and allied activities. This industry of financial direction forms the source employment of the third migration, as the farm did of the first migration, and the factory did of the second. As the first two migrations have been visualized respectively as an "outflow" and a "reflow," so may this third migration, in-drawing toward the metropolitan center, be visioned as an *inflow*.

The fourth migration (now beginning) consists of a series of local back-pushing movements impelled by metropolitan congestion and breakdowns. It is not, like each of the first three migrations, a quest for a new source of livelihood; it is a relocation of the populations and industries resulting from the second and third migrations—the relocation, that is, of the factory worker and the office worker. These workers have drawn too closely together, and now they are trying to draw apart with such grace as they can muster. The fourth migration is a *backflow*, the result of the "reflow" and the "inflow." To return to our analogy of flowing waters:

Suppose we build a low dam across a creek or little river and thus make a small pond enclosed within a natural depression in the river's valley. Next we build a second dam on top of the first one. Waters from the main stream and its tributaries up the valley flow down into the pond, press

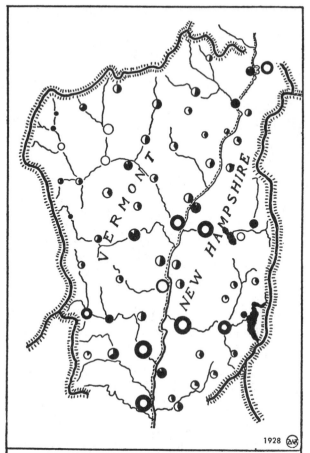

1928 ⒟ⒶⓀ

· THE INFLOW ·
(An Indication)

Increase & Decrease in Hill Towns & Valley Towns
    Upper Connecticut River Valley, Vermont &
New Hampshire. Period from 1830 to 1920. Population of whole region during whole period remains about 100,000.

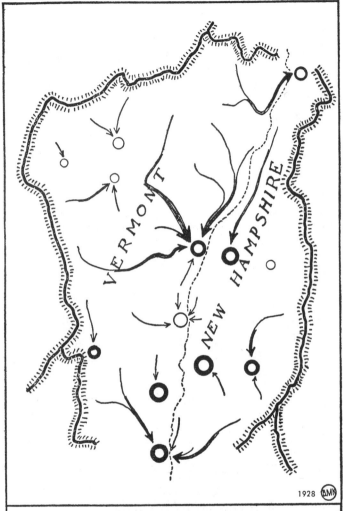

·LEGEND·

Town whose population increased from 1830 to 1920 ○
Presumable trend of population flow   1830   1920 ⟶
State boundary   ---------

·THE INFLOW·
(A Representation)

Flow of Population from Hill Towns to Valley Towns
Upper Connecticut River Valley, 1830 to 1920.

1928

against the new dam, and begin to rise. As the tide thus rises on the dam, the water extends its surface back up the main valley and up along the tributary streams. The new pond thus formed begins to branch out in fingerlike projections. The waters of the valley are, for the time being, moving in two opposite directions: first, they are moving inward as stream currents from the various sources toward the dam; and second, they are moving backward in a rising tide from the dam toward the sources. The flow of the various stream currents downward and inward forces a flow of a tidal character upward and backward. Similar movements due to similar causes have taken place in the flow of the American population. Instead of a low dam resulting in a small pond, there is a factory built, resulting in a small manufacturing town. Next a second dam is built—not a dam to collect water but to gather the unemployed: it consists of an office building alongside of the factory. Portions of the population in the tributary regions flow down into the town and press into the office building in search of jobs, causing the population of the town to rise. This pressure, continuing, in due time forces the population to extend back into the surrounding areas and along the main highways. The new city (or metropolis) thus formed begins to branch out in fingerlike projections. The populations of the region are, for the time being, moving in two opposite directions: first, they are moving inward like stream currents toward employment in factory and office; and second, they are moving backward like a rising tide away from the center of high pressure. The inward flow of population forces the backward flow.

Just such a backward flow of population is taking place in the region around Boston. Between 1915 and 1925 the population of the central wards either decreased (in one ward more than 25 per cent.) or only slightly increased (not over 10 per cent.), while that of the outlying wards (Dorchester, Hyde Park, West Roxbury, Allston, and others) increased from 10 up to 80 per cent. and more. Between 1910 and 1920 the metropolitan district outside Boston increased 19 per cent., while the city proper increased only 12 per cent. While the bulk of rural territory within a radius of 25 miles from the State House remained about stationary in population the towns along the thoroughfares increased by good percentages, and a map of the situation shows the tide of population flowing verily in fingerlike projections along the main rail lines towards Lynn, Wakefield, Woburn, Lexington, Waltham, Dedham, and the other satellite cities in the immediate hinterland. Other metropolitan centers show a similar increase in the suburban areas, and a slowing up of growth in the central district: for New York, the figures are about 18 per cent. for the city and over 27 per cent. for the metropolitan district outside; for Philadelphia, 18 per cent. and 34 per cent.; for Detroit, 113 per cent. and 255 per cent.; for Chicago, 24 per cent. and 76 per cent.; for Cleveland, 42 per cent. and 108 per cent.; for Seattle, 33 per cent. and 131 per cent.[2]

A substantial portion of this backward-flowing population consists, in the case of most cities, of commuters who make the daily trip into the central congested sections. Thus two-thirds of the daytime population of lower Manhattan Island moves in and out of that section daily. But the factories and the offices are making their exits also.

[2] From address by Mr. Gordon Culham, Greenfield, Mass., Oct. 4, 1927.

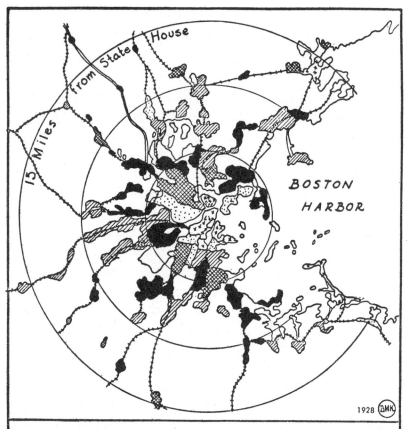

From State House

15 Miles

BOSTON
HARBOR

1928 AMK

· LEGEND ·
Relative Increase and Decrease of population
1910 to 1925

Increase,   Decrease,
0 - 10%   0 - 10%
10 - 20%   10% +
20 - 30%   Railway
30% +   Motor Way

· THE BACKFLOW ·
(A Sample)

Flow of Population from Center to Outskirts of a Metropolis. Boston Metropolitan District, 1910 to 1925. Another name for "backflow" is "metropolitan flow."

It just costs too much to poke around all day in the congested areas when, as in Manhattan, 30 per cent. of the truckman's day is spent in waiting to cross the street. No wonder horse trucks are replacing motor trucks in the downtown sections. Indeed the impelling reason for the backward flow (and the fourth migration) is not common sense and a determination to live in a more seemly environment, but simply that the centralized city is getting to be a physical impossibility. The reason lies in what Mr. Clarence S. Stein cites, in the case of New York, as "a series of breakdowns." He cites four of these.[8]

The first, historically, of New York's breakdowns was that of housing. A housing shortage and slum area had developed by 1835 and then started one at least of the earliest American metropolitan "backflows"—proceeding up the length of Manhattan Island, and submerging in time the quaint little colonial villages of Greenwich, Chelsea, and Harlem. But, says Mr. Stein, "New York has never caught up with its original shortage." The backflow, therefore, amounted to a running away from the problem rather than a solving of it, for the point of saturation has ever been maintained.

The second breakdown was that of the water system and the sewers. Mr. Stein points out the increasing danger of typhoid due to sewage contamination in the Harbor and adjacent bathing resorts and oyster beds. He says:

In 1842 New York was compelled to push back into the Croton watershed for a sufficient supply of clear water, and by the beginning of the present century the shortage threatened so acutely that a new system was planned, with reservoirs in the

[8] "Dinosaur Cities," by Clarence S. Stein. *Survey Graphic*, May, 1925.

Catskills and the Adirondacks. . . . Through this continual reaching back for new water supplies New York City is draining away, quite literally, an essential resource from other communities, dependent upon their immediate supply.

The third breakdown was that of the street system:

Our older cities were planned for four-story buildings at most. With the rise of the six-story building in the middle of the last century, traffic difficulties were felt in the shopping district of lower Broadway. An experimental safety bridge was even built. . . . Today from two to six cities have been piled up one above the other. This would be bad enough if only foot traffic and public vehicles were considered: the automobile has added the proverbial last straw. . . . If our avenues were wide enough to carry comfortably the present and potential load of traffic, there would not, in a great many parts of the city, be room for the buildings themselves.

Our city officials and engineers are now hinting that the "solution" lies in building overhead streets. But even if it were conceivable . . . this could be done only at a cost which would fall back upon the land in the shape of taxes—and in turn this would make it necessary to build higher buildings and more streets! To call this circle vicious scarcely does it justice.

The fourth breakdown is that of transportation. This, says Mr. Stein, "follows hard upon the collapse of the street system; the same causes are at work. As the city increases in height, it increases also in area; for the railroad and subway must be introduced." He goes on to show another circular dilemma: that in any scheme to inject an increasing population from surrounding regions into a central area, increased congestion inevitably demands more transport lines, and these in turn, by increasing the suburban area and its commuting population, tighten the congestion at the center.

Half a million dollars a day is the cost of congestion in Manhattan, as estimated in a traffic report quoted by Mr. Stein.[4] The great city, says Mr. Stein, "lives in the midst of a sort of perpetual cataclysm. The great city . . . is like a man afflicted with hardening of the arteries. . . . The little city that has adopted a program of mere expansion—and where is the little city that does not boast its first skyscraper?—is headed in the same direction."

The little city is in the "little pond" stage: the *inflow* is the dominant movement; the third migration is still under way. The great city is in the "big pond" stage: though the inflow is still on, the tide of the *backflow* is fast rising to meet it, impelled as it is by the crushing, breaking pressure at the "dam," which Mr. Stein so graphically describes.

The Metropolitan America we now can visualize as a moving dynamic force making its way in various directions over the map of the United States. It represents the total result of four definite flows of population:

(1) The *Outflow* led by the covered wagon.

(2) The *Reflow* led by the iron horse.

(3) The *Inflow* attracted by the skyscraper.

(4) The *Backflow* forced by pressure from the skyscraper.

Each one of these flows, to greater or less extent, is still going on. The Outflow, though no longer led by the picturesque covered wagon, continues to fill the gaps still left in the potential agricultural areas of the West. Al-

[4] Report on the highway traffic problem by Goodrich and Lewis for the Committee on a Regional Plan for New York and its Environs, 1924.

though the number of farmers in the country shrank during the past decade (1910 to 1920) by more than 15 per cent., the area of improved farm land increased by more than 5 per cent. This increase was accomplished chiefly in the prairies of the Great Plains and Rocky Mountain States and through the reclamation of arid and swamp and cut-over lands in various sections of the country. If one would see a replica of the "stump lands" frontier of the Ohio Valley of the 1820's, he can find it today on what remains of that frontier in the cut-over region of northern Wisconsin and Minnesota. The Reflow, though no longer wholly led by the iron horse over new railway trackage, is detected in the shifting of the iron and steel and other factories from the water-power sites of the New England and Middle Atlantic States to the manufacturing towns of the great bituminous regions of West Virginia and Illinois and other Appalachian and Central States. While the total of America's labor force increased during the past decade by 9 per cent., the number of manufacturing and mechanical workers increased by 22 per cent., showing thus the continued lure of the factory as a source of livelihood. The Inflow is still under big headway in all sections of the country, as is daily pointed out, and the attraction of the skyscraper is shown by an increase of the nation's clerical force by more than 82 per cent. The Backflow may be seen by visiting the outskirts of any one of our "great cities," as we have already indicated in the case of Boston.

An interesting illustration of the results of the first three migrations occurs in the region drained by the upper Connecticut Valley between Bellows Falls, Vermont, and Woodsville, New Hampshire. The population of this region taken as a whole remained almost stationary for nearly a hundred years, decreasing from 102,000 in 1830 to 98,000 in 1920. The factory towns on and near the main Connecticut River (Bellows Falls, Springfield, Newport, Windsor, Lebanon, White River Junction, and Woodsville) increased substantially during these ninety years, while the little back hill towns of the region decreased from 20 to 70 per cent. There is no accurate way of finding out just what lures were followed by the inhabitants of these hill towns. We know that the tide of their population reached its crest about 1830: their numbers mounted steadily up to this period from the first census in 1790, and then as steadily went down. Many of the first outgoers must have followed the covered wagon toward the frontier which in the 1830's and '40's was crossing the Mississippi Valley. During the 1840's the iron horse put in his appearance in the upper Connecticut, and in 1849 the main rail lines of the region were connected. Some of the folks at this time must have got jobs in the new wood-working factories or the tanneries then building in the valley towns which we have mentioned. Others between this time and 1880 must have followed the iron horse on his race to catch the covered wagon which during this period was traversing the great plains of Nebraska. Finally, from the 1880's onward many of them must have heard the city's call and hied their way toward "collars and cuffs" in Boston or New York. *The Rise of Silas Lapham* is typical of this period. Thus partly as "Outflow" and "Reflow," but chiefly as "Inflow," the hill-town population went its way, depleting the Indigenous to swell the Metropolitan America.

The upper Connecticut region is a sample of the up

country of New England; it is a sample of the Appalachian hinterland. The "Backflow" has not yet reached this region in full power; it has, however, laid its channels for invasion. These consist of the railway, and especially the motor way. They form the framework of the metropolitan "civilization." Back in the mountains, on the other hand, lie the hill towns which, depleted though they be, retain their colonial foundations. Behind these lie the crestlines of the major ranges. These crestlines form another framework—that of the indigenous "civilization." Here is the contact of the Indigenous and the Metropolitan Americas. Here is our problem—the control and guidance of this flowing Metropolitan America in its latest phase, the fourth migration—and the guidance in such wise as to preserve and develop the Indigenous America. In approaching this problem it has aided us perhaps to review, even thus briefly, the relation of this potent flow and force to other flows and forces within America. Also it should aid us now to review its relation to forces outside of America, and so to visualize our own local metropolitan invasions as part of a great world movement.

Chapter VII

APPALACHIAN AMERICA—A WORLD EMPIRE

The fourth American migration (the latest phase of the metropolitan invasion) is part of a world-wide movement —namely, the spread of so-called "iron civilization." Other names for this are "Western industrial civilization" and "metropolitan civilization." Although gasoline, rubber, aluminum, and copper are essential substances in the modern Western scheme of living, the basic stuff within this scheme still consists of iron. We are still in the "iron age." That country which possesses a supply of iron ore, plus the substances and energy necessary for reducing it, forms the natural home and source of iron civilization. (To develop this source requires, of course, an invigorating climate and a sturdy race.) Iron civilization, therefore, may for our purposes be visioned as a flow emanating from those countries possessing the substances above referred to. These substances (iron ore, coal, and other forms of energy) may be called the primary material ingredients of iron civilization (or metropolitan civilization).

In order to deal adequately, here in America, with this metropolitan civilization (or invasion), it is necessary to understand two things: first, the nature of certain contending forces working within the flow of iron civilization the world over; and, second, the importance of America (and especially of the Appalachian hinterland) as a realm of potential world-power wherein the contending forces promise ultimately to focus with more than national significance. As a basis for these inquiries we shall make a brief survey of the natural resources of the world, and of its peoples east and west. Let us begin by locating the primary seats and emanating sources of iron civilization as these are revealed by the presence of the iron ore and the coal and the other ingredients of this civilization. The figures given are, of course, approximate only, and are based on a cursory study of such official statistics as are readily available.

The iron ore resources of the world have been estimated roughly as 43,000 million tons. This tonnage refers to the amount actually in the ground awaiting use: the so-called "reserves." Four-fifths of this tonnage is distributed among the various countries as follows:

IRON ORE RESOURCES OF THE WORLD

Country	Central Region of the Field	Reserves (Million tons)	Per cent.
United States	(Whole country)	(8,000)	(18.7)
	Mesaba Range, Minn.	3,000	7.0
	Birmingham, Ala.	2,500	5.8
	Eastern Penna.	2,000	4.7
	(Elsewhere)	500	1.2
Brazil	Minas Giraes	7,500	17.5
France	Lorraine	7,000	16.4
Newfoundland	....	4,000	9.3
Cuba	Oriente	3,150	7.3
Great Britain	England	2,250	5.3
Sweden	Kiruna	2,000	4.7
Total accounted for		33,900	79.2

The coal resources of the world have been estimated roughly as 3,691,000 million tons. Three-fourths of this tonnage is distributed as follows:

COAL RESOURCES OF THE WORLD

Country	Central Region of the Field	Reserves (Million tons)	Per cent.
United States	(Whole country)	(1,367,000)	(31.1)
	Illinois	478,000	10.9
	West Virginia	421,000	9.6
	Colorado	336,000	7.6
	(Elsewhere)	132,000	3.0
China	Shansi	995,000	22.6
Canada	Alberta	286,000	6.5
Germany	Ruhr	228,000	5.2
Poland	Upper Silesia	192,000	4.4
Great Britain	England	189,000	4.3
Total accounted for		3,257,000	74.1

These tables show that the coal tonnage of the world is nearly one hundred times that of the iron ore tonnage. Since it takes about four tons of coal, under present smelting methods, to reduce a ton of iron ore into wrought iron and then into steel, it would require some 175,000 million tons of coal, or 5 per cent. of the total coal supply, to convert the world's iron ore into usable metallic form. This leaves 95 per cent. of the coal supply available for general heating and power purposes. As electrical methods of reducing iron ore are further developed, other forms of power than coal become available for the production of metallic iron and steel. However, since about 70 per cent. of the world's horse power, as estimated, is resident in coal, the latter remains the dominant element in the utilization of iron. Roughly speaking, therefore, the efficient utilization of iron ore within a country requires the presence of coal, and usually the two go together. However, the supposedly largest single deposit of iron ore in the world (that of the Minas Giraes region of Brazil) is practically with-

out a near-by supply of coal for its development, for South
America as a continent contains but a meager amount (less
than 1 per cent. of the world's total). Moreover, its supply
of power in general is also somewhat limited (4 per cent.
of the world's total). On the other hand China contains a
vast coal supply (one-fifth of the world's total), but only
a meager amount of iron ore (2.3 per cent. of the total).
The two places in the world where iron ore and coal go
together in large proportions are eastern North America
and Western Europe: they contain between them about 65
per cent. of all the iron ore and 40 per cent. of the coal.
In each case America has the lion's share. Here on these
two sides of the Atlantic, both inhabited by the white race,
are the homes and basic sources of "iron civilization."

But there are other "ingredients" besides iron ore and
coal. The motor vehicle is a critical part at present of
iron civilization, and this requires (besides iron) a supply
of petroleum and of rubber. The American "half" of iron
civilization is well off for petroleum: 11 per cent. of the
world's supply lies within the confines of the United States,
and 9 per cent. lies over the border in Mexico. Practically
no petroleum occurs within the home confines of any of the
big European nations. A small supply (3 per cent. of the
world's total) lies in the Balkans; a huge supply (more
than a fourth of the world's total) is comprised in the Russian Baku Region and over the border in Persia and Mesopotamia. The bulk of the world's rubber supply comes
from Ceylon and the East Indies, but Brazil promises to
become an important source of this ingredient. Electric
transmission of light and power is another critical part of
iron civilization, and this requires copper wire. There are

ample supplies of copper within the confines of the United States and of the European nations.

Wood is a fundamental ingredient of iron civilization. This resource, thus far in history, has been utilized, with minor exceptions in certain European countries, as if it were a thing deposited like coal instead of a growing thing like wheat: it has been "mined" instead of cultivated. In consequence the supplies of some countries, like China, have been exhausted, while in other countries, like the eastern United States, they have been heavily depleted. The chief remaining "deposits" of undepleted timber in the temperate zones are those of far Siberia and of the Pacific Coast of North America. The tropical forests remain largely intact, and the largest ultimate supplies of tropical woods will probably come from Brazil and from India and Indo-China. Forestry or timber culture must ultimately replace lumbering or timber-mining, and then wood as a resource will be measured in terms of yearly forest growth instead of, as now, in terms of current standing timber. Measured in terms of potential yearly growth, the most "fertile" forest region of the temperate zones appears to be the eastern United States, the nucleus of which consists of the Appalachian mountain area. Siberia seems to come second on the list, and then the Pacific Coast (United States and Canada).

Thus we may say that iron civilization is, as it were, "clothed and fed"—not alone with iron, but with petroleum and rubber and copper and wood and with other unnamed "ingredients" for completing the fabric of industrialism and the structure of society as a "material fact." But the people themselves must also be clothed and fed—and this literally. (After all, man needs food as well as the machine.) For food and textiles the American half of iron civilization is far better off than the European half. America, as we have seen, started as an agricultural nation: she has a bountiful capacity for the growth of wheat and beef and of cotton and wool, a capacity sufficient for her own needs and for helping out Europe. Indeed three-fifths of the world's cotton is supplied from the region from Virginia to Texas. But the countries of Western Europe, though growing enormous quantities of these staples (except cotton), must still depend on outside lands: for their wheat, on America, India, and Russia; for their beef, on these countries plus Argentina; for their wool, on the Near East and the far southern countries (Argentina, South Africa, and Australia); for their cotton, on America, Egypt, and India.

Here, then, is a way of life provided for what are called the Western peoples of the world. They comprise a quarter of the earth's population—about 19 per cent. being in the countries of Western Europe and only 6 per cent. in the United States. How about the other peoples? In almost spectacular contrast to the Western folk are the inhabitants of the bounteous valleys of China and India and the other Eastern countries. Theirs is a civilization not of iron, but rather of rice and cotton, with ideas about the universe as distinct perhaps as the physical staples on which their life seems to be dependent. These Eastern peoples comprise in numbers about half the human race. They and their countries form at present the strongholds of the "non-iron civilizations." Except for Japan, which has been partly inoculated by the desires of the West, the Eastern folk have not yet been assimilated ("benevolently" or otherwise) through the inroads of the iron horse or the other intrusives from Europe and America. Midway between the East and West, in temperament if not geography, we have the Russians. These are a land people and a northern people: a bridge from West to East across Siberia; a combination of Nordic, Slav, and Oriental; a people whose ideas and traditions of social integration have come to the surface as in no other country. They form 6 per cent. of the human race. Another 6 per cent. of human importance beyond their numbers, are the Negroes in Africa and throughout the world.

If now a resident of the planet Mars should appear and look us over, he would be likely to consider us as living on a ball of varied hues and interests, and might well in his cosmic innocence believe that said hues and interests would maintain themselves indefinitely, each in its own sphere. He would not understand at first why one in particular of these interests should start suddenly (overnight as it were) to "flow" in its iron might over, in, and through the other lands and interests of our Earth. To the sophisticated native of this Earth, however, it should require only a few reminders to see why the combination of resource, race, and climate which we have called "iron civilization" must inevitably, under present motives to action, start and wander on its way. What are the forces making for the *flow* of iron civilization? They may be briefly stated.

Perhaps the most fundamental force tending toward the "flow" of iron civilization is that of a stimulating climate, leading as it does to the development of an energetic race. On this point I can do nothing better than quote what Professor William Morris Davis has to say on "climate and man."

Those parts of the torrid zone that have a moist climate support a luxuriant plant growth and contain a great variety of animals; but they are not favorable to the development of the civilized races of man. In dry deserts and in the polar regions it

1928

·LEGEND

○ EASTERN ● WESTERN ⊗ TROPICAL ⊘ RUSSIAN ⊙ JAPANESE

RELATIVE STRENGTH OF CIVILIZATIONS

IN TERMS OF POPULATION

This map shows for each civilization (by size of circle) the present actual relative number of people (the "flesh and blood" of civilizations).

is so difficult to gain a living that human progress is hindered. As a result of the generally small land areas of the south temperate zone the great ocean preserves a uniformly inclement climate, under whose depressing influences man finds little opportunity for development.

In those parts of the spacious north temperate lands where the climate is neither too dry nor too severe, there is the great advantage of a winter that is cold enough to require the storage of food, and of a summer that is warm enough to provide the food to be stored. There can be little doubt that the habits of industry and thrift here made necessary, but not too difficult, have been of great importance in bringing civilization out of savagery.

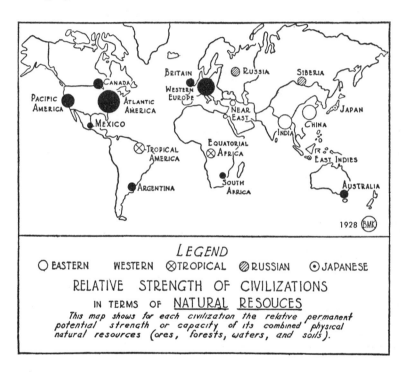

LEGEND

○ EASTERN   WESTERN   ⊗ TROPICAL   ⊘ RUSSIAN   ⊙ JAPANESE

RELATIVE STRENGTH OF CIVILIZATIONS

IN TERMS OF <u>NATURAL RESOUCES</u>

This map shows for each civilization the relative permanent potential strength or capacity of its combined physical natural resources (ores, forests, waters, and soils).

Professor Davis here shows in a few simple words just why it is that of all portions of earth it is the "spacious north temperate lands" which form the natural seats of the scheme of life called "civilization" as opposed to that of savagery. And if there is one portion of these north temperate lands more favored than the rest, it is the territory of Western Europe, for this is the only extensive region on the globe which escapes the extremes of winter cold and summer heat. (The average January temperature remains above 30 degrees, while the average July temperature remains below 80.) This salubrious temperature applies to narrow areas on the Pacific Coast (from California to British Columbia) and to portions of the North Atlantic States, but to no other regions of the north temperate zone. India for the most part is a tropical country; most of China suffers an average July temperature of 80 degrees and above, while, in addition, the northern portions must resist a January temperature of 30 and below. All of the regions named, however, except for the Rocky Mountain States of America, enjoy a moderate but not excessive rainfall.

Add to these climatic advantages of the European continent a combination of fertile lands and extensive forests, as well as the mineral stores which we have mentioned, and we seem to have a physical basis for what one historian has referred to as "the infinite variety and restless change which has characterized the institutions and fortunes of European states ever since the commencement of the civilization of our (European) continent."

Here, then, in this simple reaction between climate and man, we see what appears to be the primary force in impelling the extension and *flow* of iron civilization beyond its first home realm on the European continent. But the particular stimulus for this extension—the first impelling cause—has consisted in the European's desire for trade. This persistent desire for delivering goods in exchange for foreign treasure or other coveted reward is seen in historic and dramatic relief when, with the fall of Constantinople in 1453, the bars were placed against the trade lanes to

the East. "History," as we have already quoted Hildebrand, "became a sudden stream of purpose. The world
awoke—and started." Blocked at one door, the pressure of
restless European energy sought outlets beyond the seas.
The "stream of purpose"—first for trade and later for
humdrum livelihood—resulted in the various streams of
European civilization pushing toward the corners of the
earth. We have mentioned the parts played by da Gama,
Columbus, and Magellan, and later on, in our own country, by the march of the covered wagon. Thus, by means of
the lumbering vehicles of sailing vessel and ox team, the
"flow" got underway.

And then, only a century or so ago, another vehicle
turned up. Through the efforts of Watt and Stephenson
and other mental navigators the power of steam was applied to the revolving wheel in factory, in ship, and on the
roadway. The iron horse outstripped the covered wagon
on the American plains, as we have seen; and the steam
engine replaced the water wheel in the English factory.
The flow of "civilization" took a lunge forward—in America, in India, in Argentina, in Africa. We have traced this
lunge briefly in America, in connection with the iron horse
and the second (or manufacturing) migration. "Iron"
civilization became "steam-iron" civilization. And then
what? The vehicle takes on auxiliaries—right now in our
own generation. It takes on the electric transmission wire:
steam power is snapped on anywhere desired within a
radius of three hundred miles (and water power thereby
is reënstated). The pneumatic tire is invented, and the
internal-combustion engine, and gasoline is reduced from
crude petroleum: result—a brand-new vehicle, the motor
car. "Steam-iron" civilization becomes "gasoline-electric-

steam-iron" civilization. Thus the *flow* takes another "lunge." The metropolitan invasion is shrieking on its way.

These mechanical devices, plus certain others (the Bessemer furnace and the various ingenuities of modern metallurgy), coming "overnight," are having seemingly an effect on the potentialities of iron civilization similar to that of a sudden deluge of water upon the potent mass of a molten subterranean bed of lava. The effect is, in a word, *volcanic*. It has aspects of a "boiling over." The various flows of iron mechanism proceeding with increasing speed from the "volcanic areas" of Europe and America outward toward the "backward countries" of the East and South appear to constitute that "expansion" to which Spengler refers as the concluding winter stage in the cycle of a society. Should the curve of acceleration maintain its present trend the "springtime" of a future cycle (or else enduring chaos) would almost seem to be at hand within another generation. It happens, however, that these flows have within them certain contending forces which may delay this hour. But these forces in themselves may bring a chaos of their own. What are these forces?

First: *The "Bottle-Neck."* We have already described the great city as a conflux of traffic streams (or commodity streams). We have quoted from the vivid description of this phenomenon given us by Mr. Clarence S. Stein with respect to its causes and results, and should know the reason why he likens it to a man "afflicted with hardening of the arteries" and to a person who "lives in the midst of a sort of perpetual cataclysm." The great city is to the commodity stream what the Hoosac Tunnel is to the stream of loaded freight cars and what the neck of the bottle is to the flow of liquid passing through: it is the narrowest portion of the channel through which the stream must pass. It is, therefore, the critical portion of the outward structure or framework of industry and of industrial civilization. In case of trouble elsewhere in the framework—whether from war, or railway strike, or even a recurrence of the snow blizzard of '88—the breakdown, if such there be, must occur here in the weakest link. The "Bottle-Neck," as evidenced in the great city, is the Achilles heel of iron civilization; its potential weakness amounts to a contending "force" against the flow of this civilization.

Second: *War*—"*in posse* and *in actu*." William James in his great essay, "The Moral Equivalent of War," makes the point that "war and peace are the same thing—now *in posse*, now *in actu*." The constant potentiality of war, whether or not in actual operation, which is an inherent part of the flow of industry in the hands of rival groups, is an incessant source of weakness which, like the Bottle-Neck, one must figure as a contending "force" against the flow of iron civilization. We need only look back to the year 1914. The *occasion* of the Great War was human fear, no doubt—"the ambition of Germany" from one side, "the ambition of Britain" from the other. But underneath all this, as admitted freely on both sides both then and now, the *cause* lay in the flow of iron civilization under rival auspices from the "volcanic area" of Europe outward toward Africa, India, and the East. Though war *in actu* makes a "boom" and stimulus to industry and increases severalfold the efficiency of industrial operation, yet war—whether *in actu* or *in posse*—by diverting material and men to its own upkeep and plant, and through its demoralizing aftermath, seems to have the net effect of sabotaging the flow of iron civilization.

Third: *Worker vs. Owner*. As the flow of industry is carried on under the auspices of rival groups in different countries, so also, with the exception of agriculture, it is carried on by rival groups within each country and in each plant. One group is formed of the owners of the plant, while the other is made up of the users of the plant. The owners, or capitalists, are supposed to get their share of industry's product through an account called *profit*, while the users, or workers, are supposed to get their share through an account called *wages*. Since each account can be increased ultimately only at the expense of the other, the two groups are in perpetual rivalry. The result is the strike on the one side and the lockout on the other, plus a multitude of further devices invoked by both sides to stay the flow of industry and its iron civilization.

Fourth: *Indigenous vs. Metropolitan*. The three sets of forces just enumerated come, each of them, from within the flow itself of iron civilization; in addition to these there is a force contending from without—a frontal opposition, as it were, on the part of an indigenous culture to the intrusion of a foreign exotic influence. Western iron civilization from the first has had to fight its way against this indigenous opposition, which thus far, however, has been comparatively weak. The indigenous civilization of the North American Indian was no match for that of the iron horse or of the covered wagon, nor could the early cultures of Mexico or Peru stand up against the forces of Cortez or of Pizarro. These peoples have been in part assimilated, in part annihilated. The Negroes of Africa are now being held in abeyance through cunning instigation of intertribal jealousy. Opposition in India has been marked and open but has been readily suppressed, in terms of physical satisfaction, through cannon mouths and Gatling guns at Sepoy and Amritsar. The Philippines, in the classic words of President McKinley, have been "benevolently assimilated." Japan bowed to Commodore Perry and agreed to play the merry Western game of industrialism. China in the past has been restive and peevish at being railroaded and uplifted in ways to suit the foreign devil, and judging from recent events beginning at Shanghai, the invasion of metropolitanism is perhaps about to meet an indigenous force which, light in iron but heavy in man power and national tradition, may turn out to be an invincible opposition to what has appeared to be an irresistible flow.

Such appear to be the main contending forces affecting the flow of iron civilization throughout the world. How do these affect our problem in dealing with this flow here in America, and especially in the Appalachian hinterland? Before attempting an answer to this question we shall make some brief comparisons between America and the other countries of the earth with regard to the chief ingredients of iron civilization and to supplies of food and clothing.

First we shall compare the whole continent of North America (including its adjacent islands) with the other continents:

North America here is shown to exceed all the other continents in the percentage of each ingredient except in that of petroleum. The Near East (including the oil fields of Roumania, Persia, Mesopotamia, and the Russian Baku region) contains the largest proportion of this mobile re-source—30 per cent. of the world's total. North and South America together, however, contain nearly half the world's supply.

The bulk of North America's natural resources are contained within the United States. This nation consists physically of two quite distinct countries—of Atlantic America and of Pacific America. These are separated by the broad

CHIEF INGREDIENTS OF IRON CIVILIZATION BY CONTINENTS

	Iron Reserves	Coal Reserves	Petroleum Reserves	Potential Horse Power (All sources)	Potential Forest Growth
The world					
Total percentage	100	100	100	100	100
Percentage accounted for..	97	84	100	100	88
North America	38	38	23	36	31
South America	19	—	24	4	10
Europe	34	16	—	16	18
The Near East	—	—	30	1	—
Africa	1	1	2	12	4
Asia	4	26	21	28	24
Oceania	1	3	—	3	1

semi-arid belt which occupies the Rocky Mountain States. Atlantic America includes the Atlantic Plain, the Appalachian hinterland, and the Mississippi Valley. It is penetrated on the north side by that potential arm of the sea formed by the Great Lakes. Through this channel and by way of the Atlantic seaports the various streams of traffic and commodities tend to flow toward Europe, while through the Gulf ports and by way of the Panama Canal they tend in the direction of South America. Pacific America consists of the comparatively narrow belt west of the Sierra and Cascade ranges from which the lines of traffic and communication front in the direction of the Orient.

These two Americas (the Atlantic and Pacific), though isolated, excel any other nation, or group of nations, in general access to the world. Measured in terms of this access, or in terms of the ingredients of iron civilization, or in those of agricultural capacity, the combination of Atlantic and Pacific America seems to form potentially by far the most powerful material unit of any society which has—or can—inhabit the earth. It is a double-barreled industrial power. It fronts the East on its western side and the West on its eastern side.

Atlantic America alone is a powerful, if one-sided, geo-economic unit, and we shall now compare it with the other single countries of the world with respect to the ingredients of iron civilization.

ATLANTIC AMERICA COMPARED WITH OTHER COUNTRIES IN
INGREDIENTS OF IRON CIVILIZATION

Percentage of World Supply

	Atlantic America		Foreign Country of Highest Percentage In Europe		In the World	
	Per cent.	Country	Per cent.	Country	Per cent.	Country
Iron Ore	17.5	France	16.4	Brazil	17.5	
Coal	22.6	Germany	5.2	China	22.6	
Petroleum	7.3	Baku Region	12.0	Baku Region	12.0	
Horse Power (All sources)	19.5	Germany-Austria	4.5	China	20.0	
Forest Growth	15.0	Russia	8.0	Siberia	13.0	

The figures in this table tell their own story and are given merely to sum up some points which we have made. Atlantic America contains the world's most powerful combination of iron and coal, since Brazil has practically no coal with which to work its iron and China has but a meager amount of iron for its coal to work upon. The petroleum supply is only about half that of Baku, though this discrepancy could be offset by the extensive pools across the border in Mexico. The total horse power nearly equals that of China in amount but transcends it in effectiveness, owing to China's low supply of iron, to which we

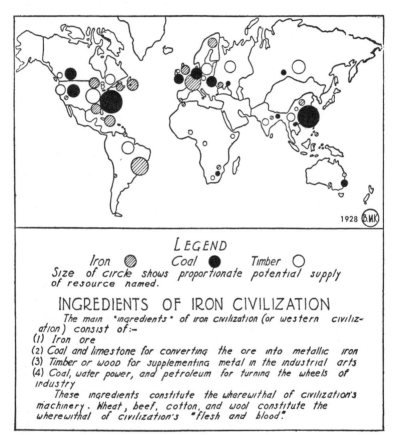

1928 B.M.K

LEGEND

Iron ⊘   Coal ●   Timber ○

Size of circle shows proportionate potential supply of resource named.

INGREDIENTS OF IRON CIVILIZATION

The main "ingredients" of iron civilization (or western civilization) consist of:—

(1) *Iron ore*
(2) *Coal and limestone for converting the ore into metallic iron*
(3) *Timber or wood for supplementing metal in the industrial arts*
(4) *Coal, water power, and petroleum for turning the wheels of industry*

These ingredients constitute the wherewithal of civilization's machinery. Wheat, beef, cotton, and wool constitute the wherewithal of civilization's "flesh and blood."

have referred. The potential forest growth is about equal to that of Siberia.

This array of dull statistics is not given to parade America as the greatest nation of the globe; on the contrary they are presented, if anything, to make us in America ponder our dangers. Whether we like it or not, we inhabit what seems to be potentially the most "volcanic" area in the realm of iron civilization, and the nucleus of this area is the territory drained by the waters flowing from the divide of the Appalachian range of mountains. This territory of Appalachian America, containing two-thirds of the iron and one-half of the coal of Atlantic America, with at least half of its forest growth, and bordered on both sides by agricultural lands which can be doubled in capacity, is a world-empire in itself. Here promise to be focused, under stupendous pressure, the various contending forces inherent in the flow of iron civilization; here if anywhere on earth will be required utmost vision if human society is ever to be guided to aught but "material fact." In what ways do the contending forces show themselves in Appalachian America?

The *"Bottle-Neck"* shows itself in ways already set forth. We have perhaps in America the most glaring instance on earth of this phenomenon—that product of the third and fourth migrations (of the "Inflow" and the "Backflow") which has intrenched itself around the strategic harbor of New York. This metropolitan district with its eight millions of people is said to form the largest single body of population of any equal area in the world. One-fifth of the export tonnage of the United States squeezes through its "Neck," but this is a minor fraction of the total traffic which comes and goes within this conflux. And New York is only one, as we have seen.

War, *in posse* and *in actu*, exists in Atlantic America (if not strictly within the Appalachian hinterland) between the various contending commercial interests, though happily there seems to be no danger that it will ever take on military form. There are a number of such "wars," but one instance will suffice. This consists of the "controversy" over the proposed deepening of the ship canal around the St. Lawrence River rapids below Lake Ontario. The deepening of this canal for ocean transit, as proposed, would round out nature's seeming plan to make of the Great Lakes series a projection of the sea. In favor of this plan are the potential seaports on these Lakes, or rather the commercial groups which operate therein. Against the plan are the rival groups working through New York harbor and the Atlantic seaports. Were the Middle Atlantic States under one political flag and the Lake States under another, we should have in a fashion a replica of the situation of the British Isles and Germany: the interests of an interior region demanding their outlet to the sea, and the interests of a seaboard resisting such demands. It would be the flag as it were of the New York Central against that of the Chicago, Milwaukee & St. Paul.

The struggle of *worker vs. owner* in America is as tense and bitter probably as in any other country. These opponents are respectively represented, in a rough and ready fashion, by the American Federation of Labor and by the National Association of Manufacturers. Groups of a more militant character are seen in the Communists on the one hand and the coal and steel operators on the other. The conflict consists for the most part of the dull, hard grind of collective bargaining between the union and the company, with frequent picturesque strikes and occasional dramatic conflagrations (as at Homestead, Calumet, Ludlow, Everett, and Passaic) which show in sharp relief the most human of the volcanic forces making up our iron civilization. There is no contingent in America equivalent to British labor, but the low-voiced Brotherhood of Locomotive Engineers, plus the yet unorganized American technicians of whom Thorstein Veblen writes, possess a key position and a constructive latent power which, in case of permanent rupture at the "Bottle-Neck" or elsewhere within the iron framework, might serve to stay a headless chaos and bring an order founded on a purpose.

The dormant conflict of *indigenous* vs. *metropolitan* is as prevalent in America as it is in China; and it is as deep-seated in the American citizen as is the labor conflict in the American proletarian. But it is almost wholly *a subconscious conflict*. The metropolitan invasion of China is clearly seen, for the simple reason that it is occurring under foreign auspices and the Chinaman is loading his gun to resist the impudent intrusion. But the metropolitan invasion of America carries no national flag, and so the American citizen does not visualize it (as does the Chinaman) as a thing foreign to his own inherent country. The open conflict of worker vs. owner is a struggle for wages and hours—for bread and for *time*. The dormant conflict of indigenous vs. metropolitan is a struggle for home and for *space:* it is a struggle for a livable environment. The proletarian is conscious of his struggle and faces his opponent—and the issue: he stays and fights it out with "the owner." The citizen is unconscious of his struggle and flees from his opponent—and the issue: if he has the means he gathers up his children and tries to run away from "the city." Environment, or the *space* in which to live, is as humanly fundamental as leisure, or the *time* in which to live; but the struggle being made for "space" is as sickly and puny as the struggle made for "time" is as vigorous and violent. We seek not that the struggle for environment should ever become violent, but we do seek that it should become conscious and deliberate.

We begin now to see perhaps how the various contending forces in the world-wide flow of iron civilization affect our problem as regional planners in dealing with this flow here in America and in the Appalachian hinterland. What is the function of the regional planner, in America, with respect to each of these contending forces?

What can the regional planner do about the "Bottle-Neck"? We have already made the point, in our discussion of the Regional Plan for New York and Environs, that the conflux of the great city is an effect rather than a cause, that it partakes more of the mouths than of the sources of the streams of goods and traffic. With the causes and the sources left intact, any ameliorative regulation of the streams down toward their mouths (such as the building of new subways) is, as Mr. Stein and other regional planners have shown, more likely than not to aggravate a situation which has become acute. The only fundamental way apparently of dealing with the Bottle-Neck is to deal with the elements of which it is made up.

One main class of these elements consists of the traffic stream, or the commodity stream; and in its flow, as we have seen, there are the contending forces which lead to war or controversy. It may be the War of 1914-18 or it may be the St. Lawrence River controversy. The problem here is the regulation of commodity-flow—the guidance of each commodity-stream, within each continent and throughout the world, through the channel which is most direct from source to destination. In the tracing of these channels lies one of the functions of the regional planner, and one already pointed out. But not until the needed steps are taken, political or otherwise, for abolishing rivalry in developing these channels, can the efforts of the planner be effective. The very tracing of these channels, however, and their visualizing in the public eye, should act as a means—and a potent means—of abolishing the rivalry. Here, then, in dealing with the forces of commercial rivalry and war, as these may be dispelled through enlightened vision of an industrial situation, may the efforts of the regional planner immediately function.

There is little if anything which the regional planner can do directly with respect to the contention of worker vs. owner. This contention can be remedied only by placing industry under auspices whereby the control of equipment and the use thereof can work in unison and not at loggerheads. Some such change, somehow or other, seems bound to come about, but in the coming thus of a régime of greater order there is always the possibility of falling into greater chaos. It is only, it would seem, by a concrete and yet comprehensive vision of exact regional industrial situations that one régime could be smoothly transferred to another; and the attainment of such vision, not alone in the technician's mind but in the public mind at large, forms another immediate vital function of the regional planner.

And of first concern in any regional industrial situation is an exact vision of the ends to be achieved. These for our purposes may be placed within two classes: the geographic and the non-geographic. The tangible objectives of the second class consist of food, clothing, shelter, and leisure *time*. The tangible objectives of the first class consist of these plus the further (and complemental) goal of environment and leisure *space*. The attainment of this goal is intimately entwined in the contention which we have termed "indigenous vs. metropolitan." Here is a dormant but vital and specific conflict in men's minds: it is the subconscious effort to preserve and to develop the inherent human values of a country (on the part of all the members of a society) against that other subconscious effort to develop the mundane values of an exotic mechanized iron civilization (on the part of the proprietors of that civilization). It is a fight for space, for a place in the sun, for an environment unshadowed by the smoke-clouds of iron metropolitan industrialism—whether in China or America. Here is the *most* immediate function of the regional planner: it is for him to "take sides" in this coming conflict, and to fight, with the sharp weapon of visualization, for the intrinsic human values of his country and his world.

Appalachian America promises to be a strenuous battleground. It looms large on the map of the world. Here is the nucleus of what seems to be, potentially, the mightiest industrial empire on earth. The next generation may see in this region the greatest eruption ever of iron civilization: the "Backflows" from our metropolitan centers, big and little, may coalesce into a laval flow, or else (to change the figure) into a modern glacier whose iron fabric may do to human life and aspiration what the ice-sheet did to life in other forms. Against this world-wide movement of the "material fact," near-cosmic in its apparent fatefulness, there stands what seems to be a puny force indeed. Its tiny evidences are seen in the tame little movements to establish National Parks and Forests, to restore the realm of nature as Thoreau glimpsed it for us, to develop the realm of art through local drama, and otherwise to invoke the "spiritual form," in our society. But within this funny little seed there also lies a cosmic force. "It is a faint intimation, yet so are the first streaks of morning." It is the first lisping perhaps of the next endeavor of that eternal determination of man to win a land and world wherein to lead a life for carrying out a human evolution in lieu of an existence for satisfying the external routine of the machine. There is a dormant barbarian thrill for freedom beating beneath the waistcoat of the average citizen, and it is beginning to awaken. The immediate job of the regional planner is to prepare for this awakening—not through unconstructive and chimerical efforts on the metropolitan "Bottle-Neck," but through a synthetic creative effort back on the crestline sources where an indigenous world of intrinsic human values (and specifically an Indigenous America) awaits its restoration and development as a *land in which to live.*

We have taken a look into the history and causes which have shaped the particular contact in this country of the indigenous and metropolitan environments. We have traced the metropolitan as an American migration and also as a world-wide flow. Such, in crude outline, are the causes behind the situation with which the regional planner has to deal. What are the consequences? What can we *do* about it? What *means* shall we employ in dealing with our situation? But first of all, what are the *ends* we seek? What do we mean by a good environment, or "land in which to live"? And what do we really mean by *living?*

Chapter VIII

LIVING VS. EXISTENCE

"I am convinced," said Thoreau, "both by faith and experience, that to maintain one's self on this earth is not a hardship but a pastime. . . . Let not to get a living be thy trade, but thy sport."

We have here the essence of the meaning of *living:* to maintain ourselves on this earth not as a toil and hardship but as a sport and quest. Thoreau was convinced this could be done. Modern engineering proves it can be done. As Stuart Chase has demonstrated, half the labor effort of America goes to waste: the gradual stoppage of this leakage will cut in two our day's work and leave us free to "live." But how? Our very freedom opens a new problem. This problem is basic for the regional planner—indeed it is for him *the* basic problem, the problem of minimizing existence, or concern with the means of life, and maximizing living, or fulfillment of the ends. Let us get these terms clear.

Existence may be easily defined. (We refer to biologic or human existence and not to a metaphysical concept.) Biologic existence consists of two main facts.

First: The maintenance of organisms already born. The activity herein required consists in the main of securing a food supply: with man there is required (in addition to food) clothing, household shelter, and a certain mechanical and industrial equipment.

Second: The replacement (or increase) of organisms upon the earth. The activity involved consists in mating and in securing the equipment and care, before and after birth, for bringing the organism to maturity. With the lower orders, such as the bird species, the equipment consists of the nest; with man it consists of the house or home.

These two processes, sustenance and reproduction—both of them forms of growth—constitute what are sometimes referred to as the "raw facts" of biologic (and human) existence. They are universally familiar and obvious and require no further elucidation. We all know what it means *to exist:* but *to live?*—that is a longer story.

The word "live" is a very little word, but its thorough comprehension is something which never perhaps will be attained by our present limited human minds. And no comprehension of it can, perhaps, be attained except through an understanding of the very deep and yet simple psychologic relation which exists between such notions as "hardship" and "pastime," "trade" and "sport," and, finally, between *work* and *play*. The most lucid treatise of which I know on the distinction between work and play is that presented by Mark Twain in a certain chapter of his book *The Adventures of Tom Sawyer*. The distinction is brought out in one of these adventures, which I shall briefly recount:

Tom dwells with his Aunt Polly. Their home is in a little Missouri town on the banks of the Mississippi River. Tom returns home on Friday night covered with mud. For this crime he is sentenced by Aunt Polly to hard labor on the following day (Saturday), while the other children will be at play. The sentence consists in whitewashing the long, high front fence. The Saturday sun rises on a beautiful spring morning. Tom appears at the end of the fence, bucket and brush in hand. He starts to work. He daubs the brush along the first board and then stops to survey the "far-reaching continent of unwhitewashed fence" and sits down discouraged. The long, blank fence spells for him a virtually endless period of blank toil. Then he hears the merry voices of his schoolmates released for a day of play. They are coming his way. His troubles forthwith double. Added to the despair of slavery is the rending terror of disgrace. The world turns black. At this dark moment Tom is seized with an inspiration—"nothing less than a great magnificent inspiration." He picks up his brush and goes "tranquilly to work." Along comes Ben Rogers, the *very* boy, of all the boys, whose ridicule Tom had most dreaded. He takes in Tom's situation at a glance —or thinks he does. "Hello, old chap, you got to work, hey?" Tom keeps on painting. Ben again reminds Tom of his disgrace. Tom steps back. He surveys his work "with the eye of an artist." He makes another pass or two and then squints again. Ben becomes interested. "Say, Tom, let me paint a little." But Tom will not listen. Ben presses his case: he offers first the core of the apple he is eating, and finally the whole fruit, for the chance to take a hand. Tom ultimately relents. Other boys come, and the process is repeated. "They come to jeer but remain to whitewash." At the end of the day the fence has been painted and Tom finds himself rich, in the local juvenile currency of apple cores, broken pen-knives, crippled cats, and other forms of junk, all obtained as the price of "whitewashing privileges." . . . And Tom, in pondering upon the events of the day, discovers a great truth. It can be told in two sentences as follows:

Work is what you are *obliged* to do.

Play is what you are *not obliged* to do.

The doorkeeper in a safe and well-ordered public building, whose job perhaps is a political gift, sits with mind relaxed, tilted back in a comfortable chair. His efforts, mental and physical, are at a minimum. But he is on duty. The mountain climber on an icy peak at dawn stands with mind intent on the brink of a cliff. His efforts mental and physical are at a maximum. But he is off duty. The mild efforts of the doorkeeper are required; the strenuous efforts of the mountain climber are made for their own sake. The doorkeeper works; the mountain climber plays.

Tom Sawyer found himself up against one of the raw facts of existence. The whitewashing of the front fence was required as a part of the maintenance of the household equipment. There were two ways—two distinct attitudes—in which Tom could approach this job. He tried them both. First he surveyed the long, blank fence as an endless piece of blank and hopeless toil; and he sat down discouraged. Then he took another look: it was a look inspired—inspired by the challenge in the voices of his oncoming schoolmates; his "work" suddenly became a game. His game was to get the other boys to paint the fence. And how? By bossing them into it? Oh, no, Tom was a wise boy. *His* game was to *make* a game. And so when Ben Rogers came along, Tom surveyed the fence once more; and this time he surveyed it "with the eye of an artist." Then Ben became "inspired": *his* eye in turn became that of the artist; and so on with the other boys. At the end of the day the fence was whitewashed; the "raw fact" had been accomplished and Aunt Polly was satisfied. It might have been accomplished as the result of hard labor;

instead it was achieved as the result of art. What would have been a day of pain was made a day of pleasure; what promised to be toil was guided into free activity and culture.

What Mr. Lewis Mumford, in *The Golden Day*, says about culture, checks up with the situation we have been describing.

Culture [he says] in its many ramifications is a working over of the raw fact. Just as eating, among civilized peoples, is not a mere hacking and gnawing at flesh and bones, but an occasion for sociability . . . as important as the fact itself and works out into a separate drama, so every act tends to be done, not just for its own sake, but for the social values that accompany it: the taste, the conversation, the wit, the sociability are esthetic filaments that bind men together and make life more pleasing.

See now how this applies to the whitewashing of Aunt Polly's fence. This job of whitewashing, as handled by Tom, was indeed a "working over of the raw fact" and was not a mere daubing of paint tediously over a row of blank boards. Instead it was "an occasion for sociability"; it was certainly "*as* important (to Tom) as the fact itself"; and it worked out "into a separate drama." Every act done by each boy—each flourish of the paint-brush— was "not just for its own sake" but for the social values that accompanied it, and the sociability of the occasion constituted a series of "esthetic filaments" that bound the boys together and made their life more pleasing.

Here, I think, is a substantial foundation for a whole philosophy of work and play, or (to use more grown-up words) of industry and culture. Mark Twain's story makes it clear that there are two kinds of work: it suggests also that there are two kinds of play. Let us see if we can separate these couplets, for it may help in getting the real distinction between existence and true living.

First, there is the kind of work which we call *toil*. This is the kind of work which Tom would have made of whitewashing the fence had he not got his inspiration. By toil I mean any sort of human effort, whether physical or mental, which is devoid of inspiration and of interest in the outcome. The only interest related to toil is that of getting it over with, and if the task is performed on a daily wage basis then the only interest is that of having time pass by. Any game which is carried on for the mere purpose of "killing time" is a species of toil. Toil is fundamental in the unrest of the industrial worker. It is best illustrated in the worker whose job it is to feed some machine. Such worker becomes thereby a part of the machine. The complete machine, therefore, is part mechanical and part human. The mental life of the mechanical portion of the machine is, of course, a blank: the mental life of the human portion also tends to become a blank. Toil, in essence, is the residue of human activity from which all inspiration and mental interest has been drained. Perhaps no work, however arduous, is 100 per cent. toil; and perhaps no work, however inspiring, is wholly devoid of toil. Toil is an element in human effort: it is an unmistakable element to any one who has ever experienced a high percentage of it.

On the other hand there is the kind of work which we call *art*. This is the kind of work which Tom finally made of whitewashing the fence. Art, like toil, is an element in human effort or activity, but it is the opposite element from toil. Art, in essence, is inspiration and interest in the outcome: art is creation. We need not dwell on the definition. Many books have been written on art, and the subject is familiar to every reader. I shall have some comments of my own on this subject as we proceed in our new exploration, but all I desire to do now is to point out the important distinction between the two opposing elements which we are everlastingly combining, in our slovenly parlance, under the contradictory term of "work." This simple difference between grind and fun which Tom Sawyer and every other school boy recognizes is often forgotten by the educated grown-ups and by the keenest minds. Steinmetz said that "work was a curse." President Eliot, of Harvard, said that "work was a joy." Both were correct: one was referring to *toil,* the other to *art.* There seem to be also two opposing elements in the thing that we call "play."

There is the element in play called *recreation.* I mean this literally—the element which re-creates, or creates anew. Recreation is said to be of two sorts—active and passive. Both kinds are illustrated in the amateur drama. The actors, being amateurs, are originally "not obliged" to do their parts, and so, according to Mark Twain, they are at play and not at work; they are participating in a free activity. Likewise with the audience. The actors are supposed to form the active portion of the occasion and the audience the passive portion; the actors are said to "take part," and the audience to "take in." But is this wholly true? Does not the audience *take part* as well as *take in?* This, of course, depends upon the audience: some audiences play their full part, while others merely sit back and "imbibe." And the actors are quick to sense the difference.

There is a wonderful interaction between stage and audience: if one responds, the other responds in ever-increasing exaltation; each one is "player," and each woos the other. Or else neither one responds; then neither one is really "player," and each goes its way unsuited. But when both sides do their share and play their part, then both are really active—audience as well as actors; both are newly creating something, both are undergoing recreation. And as in drama, so in other forms; recreation that truly re-creates is at bottom *active*. Even sleep (that which "knits up the raveled sleeve of care") is active. Recreation is constructive relaxation.

Opposed to recreation there is the element in play called *decreation*. This is defined in the dictionary as "the undoing of an act of creation." Decreation is destructive relaxation. It is glaringly illustrated in any form of physical self-abuse, for this results in undoing the various acts of nature which are required to create the human body. Self-abuse, of course, requires no creative effort, physical or mental: its practice, therefore, is essentially passive, just as the practice of recreation is essentially active. The physical self-abuse of the drunkard and the wastrel is publicly abhorrent and is pretty generally understood. But mental self-abuse is very little understood. There is mental opium as well as physical; it may be gathered from the stage, the press, the movies, and from our daily thoughts. I refer not to that form of "dope" which consists of the expression of a doctrine with which I disagree. I refer instead to a condition of the human mind itself, to a certain slovenly decreative condition which I shall term "vicariousness." It is a form of mental self-abuse, and it goes to the bottom of what is meant by decreation. I shall illustrate its meaning by an act of my own; elsewhere I have given a description of this act, which may now be quoted: [1]

I once saw Douglas Fairbanks in the photoplay *Robin Hood*. The hero climbs the proverbial tower; with one arm he catches the beautiful lady as she jumps to elude the bad man's attentions; with the other he continues climbing; then deftly annihilating Mr. Bad Man, he receives embraces nobly won. It was a glorious show. Intensely I imbibed it from start to finish, transferring my personality totally and thoroughly into Douglas's rugged body. For fifty cents I had been a hero for twice as many minutes. I left the theater victorious, vicarious, and with my money's worth. Into this vivid little Utopia I had made my "get-away" from the humdrum of ordinary prosy life.

Now, as an historian of utopias has pointed out, there are essentially two kinds: the "utopia of reconstruction" and the "utopia of escape." Their names explain the wide distinction which exists between the two. During the performance of *Robin Hood* I was residing in the utopia of escape. And it may seem to the reader very harsh and absurd of me to brand such an escape as "self-abuse." But I still brand it so. It was, to be sure, a very small and innocent dose, and I cite the instance merely in order to illustrate a tendency. For the time being I was "doped"; I was content to sit passively and become then and there a big vicarious hero, rather than inspired to take the slightest step to become a real, if diminutive, hero. Such in this particular case was my own slovenly reaction. My next-door neighbor may have got an inspiration, but as for me, I was practicing a form (however mild and innocent) of

[1] "Outdoor Culture: The Philosophy of Through Trails." *Landscape Architecture,* April, 1927.

mental self-abuse: I was merely undoing and unraveling, minus the impulse of any action on my part, a creation achieved by the action of others. For my neighbor the performance may have been recreation; for me it was de-creation.

Let us examine my neighbor's mind. For him *Robin Hood* may embody the utopia not of "escape" but of "reconstruction." For him this experience of vicariousness may be a vista of constructive vital life. Perhaps he is a playwright, and he catches in a flash some elusive idea for which he has been groping. Perhaps he is an engineer, and the mere mechanics of the hero's exploits suggest valuable notions. Perhaps he is undergoing human tribulations, and the hero's winning graces suggest to him a redeeming approach to some bruised situation. Whatever it may be, provided my neighbor is endowed with constructive imagination, then "vicariousness" may have its telling part to play. The vicarious is but a form of relaxation, and, like any other of its forms, leads one way or the other, toward the slovenly in man or toward the active—according as "he thinketh." Are we stirred to bring forth the rich endowment of our potential lives, or are we lulled to accept supinely a passing thrill as final payment?

We have now cited four elements of human experience related to work and play. They are:

Toil—blank or uninspired effort.

Art—effort inspired by an interest in the outcome.

Recreation—creative or constructive relaxation.

Decreation—uncreative or destructive relaxation.

There is little or no difference between art and recreation. The difference is an academic one—between eco-

nomic obligation, directed toward a livelihood, and un-
trammeled activity, with a livelihood assured. But otherwise they amount to the same thing—to an inspired creative activity which, when sufficiently developed, will some
day wipe out the distinction between work and play. The
term *living* refers to this activity which, in the course of
evolution, must be augmented and developed to its fullest
powers. Toil and decreation, on the other hand, represent
in their respective ways the dross of human activity and
existence, and these, in the course of evolution, must
gradually but inevitably become eliminated.

In the course of evolution! The notion which I have in
mind by the term "living" is closely tied up with the
notion of evolution. Evolution seems to be the growth
achieved by those "forces" to which Huxley refers in the
last sentence of his *Introduction to the Study of Nature*—
those forces "which extend from planet to planet, and from
star to star, throughout the universe." In commenting on
this thought we made the point that this *Introduction* (this
summing up by Huxley of the scientific explorations of the
past) marked the end of a beginning—a "coming of age,"
so to speak, in human comprehension. The revelations
which came to a focus in Darwin and in Copernicus are
those of a biologic and a cosmic evolution which appear
to form two ends of a great single process of growth.
Professor William Patten of Dartmouth College uses the
term "Evolution, or World Growth." The inorganic seems
to "grow" as well as the organic. Thoreau says, "There is
nothing inorganic." We are fascinated in a way we cannot
explain in the pursuit of a comprehension of the forces (or
Force) behind the outward facts of evolution; and so we
are possessed to pursue and explore what Professor Patten

calls "those tell-tale changes in the outer world, or the messages of God, if you please." The essence of true "living," it seems to me, consists in the pursuit and exploration of these "messages" as they come to us—or as we go after them—in our affairs of science and art and recreation and love. *Living is man's part in evolution.*

Such is the "activity" for which the environment developed by the regional planner should provide. Raymond Unwin, the English architect, says that he cannot design a house until he can visualize the line of *activity* which is desired to take place therein. As with a house, so with a region. If the line of activity consists in mere *existence* and industry—the necessary routine going with the raw facts of sustenance and reproduction—then one kind of environment is called for. But if the activity consists in *living* and culture—the "working over" of these raw facts as a part of evolution—then quite another kind of environment is called for. Is it means or ends that we are after? Mr. J. S. Dwight, one of Emerson's contemporaries, once observed that "we do not properly live these days, but everywhere, with patent inventions and complex arrangements, are getting ready to live. The end is lost in the means, life is smothered in appliances." And this is why civilization is a wilderness: it is "smothered in appliances"; and so of course "the end is lost in the means." The very first act, therefore, in getting our direction for the exploration of this wilderness, is to point the telescope of our attention, and of our visualization, upon *the end*. This is the first thing to look for from the top of Mt. Monadnock.

It is necessary, therefore, that the regional planner should have from the start some definite philosophy regarding life's objectives on which his plans and explorations should be focused. Does life's objective consist in existence merely or in living? We shall assume, without arguing the point, that it consists in the activity of living; and so we shall attempt to sum up briefly those aspects of this particular activity for which our environment should provide.

Living we have just defined as "man's part in evolution," and this takes place best, apparently, in the form of that activity which we define as "culture"—the working over of the raw facts of existence. Culture seems to consist of a pursuit, consciously, of these raw facts, but a pursuit which, subconsciously and incidentally, "works out into a separate drama." The pursuit, consciously, of the raw fact of sustenance, has produced through the centuries the intricate mechanism of modern industry and the processes of applied science; it has also developed, incidentally, the separate drama of pure science and of the exploration of the outer mysteries of nature and her "telltale" messages. The pursuit, consciously, of the raw fact of reproduction and care of the young, has produced the elaborate processes of modern practical hygiene and education; it has also developed, incidentally, the separate drama of the fine arts and of the exploration (through the paths of music, poetry, and allied activities) into the *inner* mystery of nature's messages. In the development of the "separate dramas" arising out of the pursuit of these raw facts—sustenance and reproduction—man appears to have the means for taking part in evolution and for ever widening his mental and spiritual horizon. This is the immediate as well as the ultimate goal of all sound, comprehensive regional planning. If we forget this goal, human effort is a perpetual squirrel cage, in which we work to eat and eat to work: in this state, even our play loses its creative quality, and as the sign I once saw in an Indiana amusement park dismally reminded every one who entered its gates—Play Hard so you may Work Hard—all the possibilities of love, adventure, and enjoyment narrow themselves into the routine of a merely busy existence. When we remember the goal of living, even our work takes on a different character: we seek constantly to diminish the sphere of animal toil and to widen that of art; so that finally work and art and recreation and living will all be one. Regional planning is the effort to arrange the environment in such a fashion that this goal may be effectively and eagerly pursued.

Chapter IX

ENVIRONMENT AS A NATURAL RESOURCE

Environment is outward influence. It is defined as "the sum of the influences which affect an organism from without." It appears to be extrinsic rather than intrinsic. It belongs to what we call the "outer world," which appears to be different from the "inner mind." But what else is the outer world but an extension of the inner mind? It is certainly a form of life in which every inner life takes share. Environment is the influence upon *each* inner mind of the thing shared by *every* inner mind: it is the common layer of air which we all breathe—the filament which binds our separate lives. "Look out and not in," we are told, for when we look *out* we thereby look *in*—to our fellow souls on earth. Environment, therefore, provides a sort of *common mind*—the total life which every life must share: it is the least common denominator of our inner selves.

"All the world's a stage and all the men and women merely players."

Stage and players, setting and activity—these, as we have noted, are the two halves of environment. But what is a "player"? A player is one who *lives:* one who practices neither toil nor decreation but the inspired "activity" where work and play are one. "I work an hour a day," said Steinmetz, "and spend fourteen hours at engineering." Let us take the liberty of translating this remark: "I toil or do chores for an hour a day and spend fourteen hours at play, which in my case is engineering." Steinmetz was a "player." So was Darwin—Whistler—and Wordsworth —and Beethoven. These were big players: most of us are little players; or rather we can learn to be as soon as we learn enough to become the masters instead of the servants of our industrial machines. This kind of playing—the Steinmetz, Whistler, Wordsworth, Beethoven variety— constitutes that sort of activity which we call *living*. Stage or setting plus such activity constitute the kind of environment sought in our new exploration: it is the environment to Mother Earth and God's Nature; it is *environment, the natural resource.*

And this is nothing less than the *indigenous environment*. Indigenous is defined as "innate, inherent, intrinsic." Isaac Taylor said that "joy and hope are emotions indigenous to the human mind." The three elemental environments which we have cited (the primeval, the communal, and the urban) appear to be, like "joy and hope" themselves, "indigenous to the human mind." So it is the indigenous environment, and no other, which constitutes the *natural resource.*

The indigenous environment is, as we have stated, a psychologic resource. It is one of the energy resources. Energy is converted from a potential to an actual condition in three ways: mechanical conversion, biologic conversion, psychologic conversion. Let us consider them.

Mechanical conversion is illustrated by the water wheel or turbine; it can be illustrated also by the process of burning coal under a steam boiler. Coal consists of wood formed in the luxuriant forests of the carboniferous age. Wood is "bottled sunshine" or bottled solar energy, which, through burning, is converted first into heat, next into steam pressure, and finally into actual motion. Thus the energy which in the coal heap of the locomotive-tender lies dormant and inevident is rendered sensible and evident in the moving train of freight cars. The energy as shown in the moving freight cars is easily perceived by the human senses—of sight, of sound, of contact—and so we call it "actual." The same energy when reposing in the coal heap is not outwardly perceived by any of the senses, but we can figure it out as a possibility, and so we call the energy "potential."

Biologic conversion is illustrated by the process of absorption which takes place in the leaves of trees. We have said that wood is "bottled sunshine." The "sunshine" or solar energy is bottled in the tree trunk through this process of absorption. The leaves, under the action of the sun's direct rays during the summer growing season, take from the surrounding air a certain gas (carbon dioxide) and cause it to "flow" down through the twigs and branches and stem so as to form an enveloping layer of wood, or "annual ring," which surrounds the stem and each of the branches. By this enveloping and "fattening" process the tree trunk grows from year to year, the only growing part of the tree being this outer ring or layer (the *cambium layer* as it is called). As the invisible energy in a heap of coal is converted under the locomotive-boiler into the visible motion of the freight cars, so the energy in an unseen gas and the sun's direct rays is converted in the leaves into the visible substance of wood. Thus one form of latent energy (that in the sun's rays) is converted into another form of latent energy (that in the wood of the tree's trunk). Thus also is invisible matter (carbon dioxide gas) converted into visible matter (the wood substance of the tree's trunk).

Psychologic conversion of energy may be illustrated by certain processes and reactions of the human brain and mind upon the thing which we have called environment. As in the leaves and cambium layer of the tree an unseen gas is converted into visible and solid wood, just so in the cells of the human brain another sort of unseen (or obscure) reality is transformed into substantial evidence. The diffused beauty of a landscape which to the ordinary eye is obscure and perhaps inevident, is, through the brain-action and skill of the artist, captured and placed on sturdy canvas for all to see and comprehend. The elusive thrill of an early spring morning is caught by a Wordsworth or a Whitman and placed before us upon the printed page. The deeply moving rhythm which with us ordinary folks passes by unnoticed is detected by a Chopin, translated by a Paderewski, and placed within our souls to make them richer. In each case a thing of beauty is lifted from the common cerebellum of creation and made a joy forever; an unseen reality is focused to our duller senses to give them appetite for vision; the potential happiness resident in "natural setting" is rendered actual.

In all three of these ways of converting energy (the mechanical, the biologic, and the psychologic), that which is inevident and potential is turned into something which is evident and actual. In each instance also there is a *base* and a *reaction*. Coal is a base, the burning of it is reaction; carbon dioxide is a base, the absorption of it is reaction; the landscape is a base, the painting of it is reaction.

Environment, like every other natural resource, is developed by means of a reaction directed toward a base.

Another name for base is "stage" or "setting"; another name for reaction is "activity." We have noted the reaction or activity of the landscape painter; of the poet and of the musician. All of these activities are forms of art; all are carried on by "players." As the material resources and those of mechanical energy are developed by means of the various activities classed as *industry,* so the resource of environment is developed by means of the various activities of the fine arts, or *culture.* Each one of these activities develops a portion of the resource—it picks out (rightly) its own little fragment to be emphasized: but the complete development—the development of *environment as such*—requires a *synthesis* of arts. It requires more than each art working by itself; it requires all arts, working all together.

We shall in a later chapter consider the possible development of such a synthesis, but first let us look more closely than heretofore into the nature of the indigenous environment.

The most fundamental portion of the indigenous environment consists of the primeval. For the other portions (the communal and the urban) are found ultimately to be but compounds of the primeval. The primeval is "The All" of visible creation: it is the known quantity from which we came, as God is the unknown. The primeval is bequeathed to us by God alone; all other environments are bequeathed by God with man's assistance; and with man comes in the element of fallacy. Man's needs, of course, require sturdy changes in any environment which comes unmodified from "the hands of its Maker." And yet the less an environment is affected by human hands, the greater the range of human minds it unites. The unmodified environment, apparently, approaches closest to the common mind of all humanity: it is the one thing which is agreeable to all our inner minds. Some one has said that discord has no basis in eternity. It seems to have no basis in the primeval environment as it comes to us unmodified by the animal world. The primeval, on the contrary, seems to possess an innate harmony, and this must be why it appeals to us as an innate environment.

The most appealing harmony, perhaps, of the primeval is its ever-recurring youth—the opening of the springtime and the dawning of the day. The sense of eternity thus generated has been captured by Thoreau and put in simple words. He says: "I have been as sincere a worshipper of Aurora as the Greeks. . . . Morning brings back the heroic ages. . . . There is something cosmical about it. . . . Little is to be expected of that day to which we are not awakened by our own newly-acquired aspirations from within, to a higher life than we fell asleep from." And again: "Morning is when I am awake and there is a dawn in me. . . . We must learn to reawaken and keep ourselves awake, not by mechanical aids, but by an infinite expectation of the dawn."

This sentiment is concretely illustrated in the growth of a tree's stem or trunk. This grows, as we have noted, by the accumulation of concentric enveloping layers, or annual rings. The annual ring is the result of the growth of the "cambium layer" above mentioned. The cambium during the dormant months of autumn and winter consists of a thin film of potential growth awaiting the "dawn" of the spring's sunshine and loosened energy. During the months of spring and summer the fluid cambium layer, deriving its substance through the leaves from the ethereal carbon dioxide of the air, forms itself into the solid wood of the annual ring and thereby of the tree's trunk. Again, in the autumn, the cambium becomes a film of potentiality awaiting once more the "dawn." And so from year to year ad infinitum. For the cambium, left unmolested, is a thing of eternal life. It may be killed, but it will never of itself die. The cambium of an oak tree five hundred years of age is just as "young" as that of the oak sapling three years of age. The tree itself becomes in time too large to hold the cambium together, or else it is attacked by some disease, and thus the cambium is "killed." Else it would go on forever as a perennial potentiality— a force and spirit that has learned to reawaken, and *keep* itself awake, by "an infinite expectation of the dawn."

There seems to be within the primeval that measured cadence between expectation and fulfillment which goes to the bottom of all harmony. Harmony is happiness. It consists not of superlatives; neither is it made of promises: it is produced by the journey in between. It is pianissimo leading to crescendo: the potential pristine green of early April leading to the crashing red and yellow of October; the first snow flakes before Thanksgiving leading to the jovial blizzards of February; the feeling of 4 A.M. leading up to that of 4 P.M.—and then, with taps and sunset, the promise of *another* day and of a higher life than the one we fall asleep from. "To him whose elastic and vigorous thought keeps pace with the sun, the day is a perpetual morning." "Morning" consists of one dawn plus the expectation of another; "morning" is a continuing symphony —the onward march of primeval nature.

The opposite of symphony is cacophony. Symphony seems to be an inherent quality of all creation; cacophony comes as an intruder on creation. Both things occur within the primeval world: symphony is indigenous to the primeval world, but cacophony is intrusive or exogenous. In this the animal kingdom is chief offender: the sentient beings of creation have been the breakers of the peace. The struggle for existence is a story of cacophony, and the higher we go in the animal scale, the greater seems to be the discord. The struggle throughout concerns the raw fact of sustenance; with the higher animals it concerns, in addition, the other raw fact of reproduction. The robin apparently selects his mate without collision or other discord and sings his merry springtime song as part of nature's symphony. But bull moose have the habit of fighting to a finish for possession of the female, and the remains of their locked horns give evidence of the fierce futility of their cacophony. The simian is probably the very worst of all the animals in his sins against creation, and man is the worst of all the simians. The story of Adam and Eve, though false in fact, is profound in truth. Man's cacophony has developed around both classes of raw facts —sustenance and reproduction: it relates to two main problems: (1) that of *sustenance and industry;* (2) that of *reproduction and the home.* The first problem is a portion of the struggle for existence; the second is this plus an attempt toward the attainment of real living. Let us take a look at each.

The cacophony attending man's struggle for existence and his development of industry has been so blatant and notorious as to give the impression that it is desired for its own sake. War is the only part of business which has been set to music. This is because the cacophony of battle is so precise a replica of hell that symphony must be resorted to as a syrenic means to lure men into it. Truly stirring rhythm is thus developed along with imbecilic war-cries; art as pure emotion is advanced along the right of way, while reason and perspective are side-tracked for a quieter day. But aside from war, the cacophony of business and industry is seldom camouflaged so far as outward aspects go. The hideousness of business and industry, both in the producing and the sales departments, is left exposed in all its nakedness, from the grimy, smoke-belching factory of the industrial suburb to the notorious billboard along the motor road. This apparently sought-for cacophonous environment applies not only to the industrial plants themselves, but to the stabling and housing of their workers. A vivid picture of this "lust to make the world intolerable" is presented by Mr. H. L. Mencken in a recent essay on "Hideous Steel Towns of Pennsylvania." Here are some significant passages:

The other day, coming out of Pittsburgh by train, I rolled eastward for an hour through the coal and steel towns of Westmoreland county. . . . Here was the very heart of industrial America, the richest and grandest nation ever seen on earth— and here was a scene so dreadfully hideous, so intolerably bleak and forlorn, that it reduced the whole aspiration of man to a sort of joke.

The country itself is not uncomely. . . . But [it contains] the most loathsome towns and villages ever seen by mortal eye . . . as if some titanic and aberrant genius, uncompromisingly inimical to man, had devoted all the ingenuity of hell to the making of them. . . . It seems incredible that mere ignorance should have achieved such masterpieces of horror. There is a voluptuous quality in them. They look deliberate.[1]

[1] "Hideous Steel Towns of Pennsylvània," by H. L. Mencken. *Boston Herald*, Sunday, January 23, 1927.

Mr. Mencken pictures other striking instances—here in the mighty world-empire of Appalachian America—of reducing man's aspiration to a joke. This situation he calls "deliberate." Well, perhaps it is. The workers dwelling in these steel towns are, as is well known, in profound rebellion against their condition in life. They and American workers generally are fighting deliberately and definitely for higher pay and for longer hours of leisure. They are fighting, incidentally and vaguely, for "better living-conditions." The demand for *time* in which to play and "live" is deliberate and articulate, but the demand for *space* is incidental and inarticulate. The average worker (and the average man or woman) oftentimes seems, to some of us, to be actually desirous of a cacophonous environment. But this probably is not really true. He merely is not ravenous for a symphonious environment; and the feeble demand for the one looks like a "deliberate" demand for the other.

The demand for a symphonious environment appears to play no serious part in the problem of *sustenance and industry:* it does, however, play the leading rôle in the problem of *reproduction and the home*. Cacophony in the home, though plentiful, is recognized as a fundamental evil, and as the one indeed which strikes at the integrity of the institution itself. The home is conceived at least in symphony. In nothing else do lovers meet. That is their whole game—to create a symphonious environment—an harmonious "common mind." But in each individual mind there are usually certain portions not common to the other fellow's: these portions (pertaining to "the one" and not "the two") sometimes trespass on the common denominator: then comes the cacophony. These trespasses vary greatly—from the little ripplings known as "lovers' quar-

rels" to the invading state of mind called "incompatibil-
ity." As with lovers, or the husband and wife, so with the
family and home: the basic desire and ambition—the sole
point of the institution—is an atmosphere and environment of mutual harmonious living; when discord comes,
as it so often does, it comes as an invader and as something
foreign to the basic stuff. As with the home, so with the
community and with human society generally: symphony
is indigenous, cacophony is exogenous.

The purely indigenous environment is essentially a symphonious environment; and it is nothing else. It is the
source and support of all true living. The indigenous environment is the basic natural resource of civilization as a
"spiritual form"; all the other natural resources (the soils,
the ores, the waters, the forests) are basic of civilization as
a "material fact." Man *lives* not by bread alone—nor by
clothing, nor by shelter. One more big category needs to be
provided: it is an extension of the category which we call
"shelter." Each one of us, each family of us, needs a roof,
and warmth, and light, and water supply, and some degree of sanitation. But it takes more than these to make a
home. Each group of us who live in the same town need
houses and stores and streets and churches and school
buildings: but it takes more than these to make a real
community. The nation as a whole needs towns and roads
and industries and a great deal of other material plant:
but it takes more than these to make a pleasant land to
live in. Mere "shelter," therefore, will not suffice. We need
a further category. This is environment: it is a particular
kind of environment—*indigenous, innate, symphonious
environment.*

The environment described by Mr. Mencken (in the

Pittsburgh region) is the very opposite of this. He describes the exogenous environment—none other indeed than our old acquaintance, the metropolitan environment. He describes it correctly—as an intrusion into the indigenous environment. The latter, "the country itself," he says, is "not uncomely," but it is invaded by "the most loathsome towns and villages ever seen by mortal eye." Mr. Mencken is describing nothing more or less than the metropolitan invasion. He describes this as something "uncompromisingly inimical" to man, as something "so intolerably bleak and forlorn" as to reduce the whole aspiration of man to "a sort of joke." We have here "the country itself" of the Allegheny Mountains—the indigenous, innate, symphonious environment—invaded by the metropolitan flood—an *exogenous, unnatural, cacophonous environment.*

As rational men and women, plainly, we would develop the one and control the other. But *how?* We have considered the ends—how about the means? And first, what precisely does the regional planner mean by "planning"?

Chapter X

PLANNING AND REVELATION

What is the essence of a good plan? I recall the words of a certain civil engineer while seated around the evening camp fire during a surveying trip into the hemlock country of western Pennsylvania. Absorbed in thoughts of the day's work, he sat gazing into the embers. Suddenly he came to life with an expression of relief: "Well, I can't help it, *I* didn't make the country!"

We were running a line for a logging railroad which was to cross a divide and dip over into an adjoining valley. We hoped the line could reach the bottom on a 6 per cent. grade. But we discovered that this could not be. The grade must be steeper, or else switchbacks must be put in. The engineer was disappointed. His first "plan" could not be carried out. The reason was that his plan did not fit nature's. Nature had molded the country in a certain way. The job of the engineer was to find out that way: it was not to inflict a plan of his own, but to uncover nature's plan. And so it spelled relief to the engineer to realize that after all it was not for him to "make the country."

"To command nature," said Plato, "we must first obey her." That is what this engineer did. He desired to command nature by locating a railroad whereby the hemlock timber could be removed from a certain valley. This he wanted to accomplish by means of a railroad having the easiest possible grade, and so he ran a line to see if he

could get into the valley on a 6 per cent. grade. He discovered that nature would not allow this. And so he
yielded to nature (he "obeyed" her) by finding another
line—a line which suited her, a line which required a
grade of 6½ per cent. instead of 6. Having made this ad-
justment, the engineer was enabled to build his railroad
into the valley and remove the timber: having thus obeyed
nature, he was able to command her.

Here we have the function of every sort of "planner":
it is primarily to uncover, reveal, and visualize—not alone
his own ideas but nature's; not merely to formulate the
desire of man, but to reveal the limits thereto imposed by
a greater power. Thus, in fine, planning is two things:
(1) an accurate formulation of our own desires—the specific knowledge of what it is we want; and (2) an accurate revelation of the limits, and the opportunities, imposed and bequeathed to us by nature. Planning is a
scientific charting and picturing of the thing (whether
logging railroad or communal center) which man desires
and which the eternal forces will permit.

The basic achievement of planning is to make potentialities visible. But this is not enough. Visibility is only part
of revelation. The mold must be rendered not only visible
but audible. It must be *heard* as well as *seen*. The regional
planner, in revealing a given mold or environment, must
portray not alone for the sense of sight, but for that of
hearing also. Indeed he must portray in terms of all the
senses. If he would portray for us a possible colonial village in New England, he must portray it in terms of the
three dimensions—and of the five senses. He must in his
imagination see the Common, and hear the church bell,
and smell the lilac blossoms, and contact the green-shut-

tered houses: he must also see and hear and contact the human activity. The individual art of painting consists in revelation in the realm of eyesight; the individual art of music consists in revelation in the realm of hearing; but the synthetic art of developing environment consists in revelation in the realm of all the senses. Planning is revelation—and all-round revelation.

The function of planning is to render actual and evident that which is potential and inevident. The potential image on the exposed camera film requires the chemical of the photographer to develop it and make it actual; the potential images and worlds lying within the surface of a region require the chemical of the imagination to develop them and make them actual. This action of the imagination has already been described under the term of "psychologic conversion." This is closely related to biologic conversion: the action of the human brain cell is akin to that of the cambium layer. The cambium is that layer of perpetual fluidity which in the tree converts the ethereal substance of carbon dioxide into the solid substance of wood and timber. It represents the realm of creative action (call it art or engineering): it represents the eternal present—that fluid twilight zone between the ethereal future and the solid past wherein our destiny is molded. Planning takes place in this cambium, twilight zone.

There are two particular potential images and worlds lying within practically every region: these are the indigenous world and the metropolitan world. The contrast between them is obscure and inevident. The *most* important revelation to be made by the chemistry of the imagination, in our own particular problem of regional planning, is the rendering evident of this inevident contrast.

The notion is dawning in the public mind, apparently, that something is wrong with the way in which our towns and countryside are being treated. The cry grows louder against "billboards," "hot-dog stands," and the "motor slum" which is pushing its way along the rural waysides. "Slum flow" is what a friend of mine has called it, a term which we might well use as a short name for "metropolitan flow." Now and again the cry strikes directly toward the contrast itself between the indigenous and metropolitan environments. Note these interesting comments made by Mr. John H. Bartlett, First Assistant Postmaster General, in his speech in Newport, New Hampshire, on the occasion of the centennial celebration of Sullivan County: [1]

An appealing cry for help comes from the small and fast-vanishing villages of our small towns and can be heard from every hilltop in the County. . . . If the present course of human events in these places continues, is it possible that we will finally have in Sullivan County only two towns, or so-called cities [Claremont and Newport]? And I conjecture that then the chain stores would prevail here—those monopolistic "strings" that are bossed by outside capital, and stocked up and cashed up by machine-made boys shot here from distant headquarters. . . . It seems to me that we are afflicted with pernicious myopia if we cannot see this tendency of things, this toboggan of events against the little villages. . . .

Concentrated business, concentrated capital, concentrated power, concentrated politics, concentrated everything! Where does this process of concentration leave the individual? And where, forsooth, does it leave the poor little town? Where does

[1] Reported in *The Boston Herald*, July 6, 1927.

it deposit the power that governs our State and shapes the destiny of our old-fashioned New Hampshire civilization?

Mr. Bartlett, a high Government official, is expressing here a deep undercurrent in public consciousness: it is an arraignment of the metropolitan mold and an appeal for the indigenous—an arraignment of "concentrated everything" and an appeal for the "New Hampshire civilization." Yet along with this desire for the innate life there goes, as Mr. Mencken has pointed out, the seemingly "deliberate" effort for the opposite—the lust (the "libido" as he calls it) to build loathsome towns and to "make the world intolerable." The confusion in men's minds regarding the underlying nature of the indigenous and metropolitan worlds is entertaining, but it is tragic. These worlds, these environments, represent in their essence the antipodes of human experience: one is inherent, the other is intrusive; one is natural, the other is mechanized; one is art, the other is artifice; one is symphonic, the other is cacophonous.

But unfortunately it is not in their essence that we experience these environments; we experience them instead in what might be called in very truth a "complex." We get the two essences in combination. The titanic turreted skyscraper viewed through evening lights from New York harbor combines national power in repose and majesty with imperialistic affront and sinister contemptuousness. The down-town shopping district of the average small American city, with its left-over shade trees, combines the home-coming thrill of the stately elm-lined village roadway and common meeting-ground with the rotary excitement of the typical Main Street. The journey by motor through the American countryside combines the elixir of the stage-coach drive through hill and dale with the melancholia inflicted by a wayside architecture glorying in the heyday of its drabness. There is a hankering lure about each one of these phenomena: there is in them, as Mr. Mencken would say, "a voluptuous quality" of almost ecstatic ugliness.

The metropolitan environment, taken as a whole, is a sort of modern inorganic siren. She is the mistress of our outreaching yet befuddled senses. We are like the man who is attracted toward a courtezan. To get an ounce of solid living he endures a pound of the meretricious. And we do likewise—those of us who "fall for" metropolitanism. If we would admire suggestion of majestic power, we must grovel before display of imperial contempt; if we would attain a little thrill of village hominess, we must submit to the blasts of Main Street blatancy; if we would snatch a whiff of verdant countryside we must tear through a stench of tenemented roadside. To get an ounce of the native and indigenous we must take a pound of the foreign and exogenous. This is so in the courtezan environment; and it is so in the metropolitan environment.

The roué endures the courtezan because she contains a tiny element of the innate woman; most of us endure the metropolitan life—the exogenous life—because it contains an element of the innate life—the indigenous life. The drop of peppermint flavors the whole of what would otherwise be a stale and flat concoction.

The revelation of a contrast (as that between the indigenous and the metropolitan) marks one fundamental aspect of regional planning. There is another fundamental aspect. This is the revelation of potential conditions in preparation for some possible occasion or event. This is best illustrated perhaps in the case of military planning, where the expected event is an emergency—something requiring immediate yet comprehensive action.

Supposing our friend the civil engineer, mentioned previously in this chapter, had been a military engineer. Supposing his problem had been, not to bring a railroad into the valley, but to bring an army in. The problems are much alike: in each case some manner of road would be required; that is, some means of access. One is an industrial problem, the other a military problem. Each requires preparation and mental forethought. Neither the railway nor the army could properly enter the valley until the scouts had gone ahead and charted (mentally) the way.

Every deliberate action—big or little, good or bad, military or industrial—starts in the mind. It must be conceived and rehearsed in the realm of thought before it can "take place" in the physical. It must be *created* before it can be *done*. So-called "doing" is only half the job.

Nobody knows this better than the military engineer, or strategist. Witness Napoleon with his maps. Not that he charts in advance each particular campaign or movement. Usually there is not time for that. But he has charted—perhaps many times—the general military situation. He has studied the ground, and the armies, and a multitude of potential actions. He has directed a dozen battles *in his mind* before he directs one battle on the ground. By thinking through the dozen battles that never do take place, he equips himself to handle the one which comes to pass.

Military strategy is one kind of regional planning. It is the charting and visualizing of deliberate, coördinated action over an extended territory. So also is industrial regional planning: it is the charting and visualizing, within a region, of coördinated action for the purposes of industry. So also is regional planning in general: the visualizing within a region of coördinated action for the purposes of general human living.

Planning with respect to expected or possible events is a matter of mental preparation: it is revelation plus elasticity. This applies to war, to industry, and to general living; it applies to a military invasion and to a metropolitan invasion. As with the small affairs of life, so with the large; all we can do is to know our mind and watch our chance. We plan for various contingencies—A, B, C, and D. *And then E happens!* Four precious plans we must cast aside, but on the *strength* of these (the knowledge attained in framing them) we can forthwith frame a plan for meeting E. We can never foresee with surety our particular actual opportunity: we can, however, if we will, foresee a series of potential opportunities. And we can prepare ourselves mentally for each. By preparing for several things which *may* happen, we indirectly prepare ourselves for what *does* happen. Planning is strategy: it is the revelation of a number of possibilities in order to control a single actuality.

Our immediate particular job, with respect to preparing ourselves mentally for the vicissitudes of the metropolitan invasion, is the charting, revelation, and contrasting of the indigenous and metropolitan molds. For into one or the other of these the future population is bound to flow. Population, like water, follows the channels that have been laid for it. That mold which is most in evidence is the one which will control the currents of the population. If, therefore, we are in favor of one mold as against the other (as we are) then it is for us to reveal that mold—to bring it out and develop it and make it strong—to make it resistant to the intrusion and the invasion of the other mold.

Before attempting (in the next chapter) a concrete charting of the indigenous and metropolitan molds, we shall consider briefly a subject closely and fundamentally related to this charting, which we have not discussed before. This is the problem of the flow of population, not merely in a single region or country, but throughout the world at large. This question is too big to take up even in outline within this small book, and we consider it at all merely to dispose of it. The problem is nothing less than *the control of the world's birth rate.*

This subject of the birth rate lies at the bottom of every social question known to man. It is obviously related to regional planning, and not only to the problems of the regional planner but to those of other "workers for the common good"—the social worker, the political reformer, the economic reformer, the labor leader. But none of these allows his particular line of evolution to wait on the solution of the riddle of population. It might be maintained that this is what he should do: that the regional planner, for instance, wastes his time when he visualizes the mold for the distribution of the flow of population, while the source of the flow itself remains unchecked. This point appears to be well taken, especially so since we are stoutly maintaining within the pages of this book that the regional planner should deal with the sources and not the "mouths" of the population's flow. Our position can be clarified perhaps by means of the same analogy which we used before—that of controlling water-flow.

A civil engineer is given the large problem, let us say, of controlling the flow of the Mississippi River and of preventing or reducing floods such as those which have made such havoc during recent years in the lower reaches of the valley. He should not, in our opinion, depend wholly on the construction along these lower stretches of revetments and levees whose only function can be to hold intact a flood wave which has already got started: he should, instead, build in the regions of the headwaters a series of storage reservoirs such as the Pittsburgh Flood Commission projected to control the floods at Pittsburgh. Furthermore, he should take steps to maintain on the upland watersheds above the reservoirs sufficient forest-cover to make for equable flowage and for reducing the process of "silting up" the reservoirs. In short, he should catch the flood wave before it gets started, by controlling the flow in the highest portions of the land.

But is this enough? Why stop at "the land"? Why not go into the sky? For the rainfall in the sky is the source of all waters on the land. But perhaps you will maintain that we know very well that man has no control of rainfall. We know nothing of the kind. It is an open question whether the maintenance of a continental forest-cover affects the continental climate. There seem to be good reasons for thinking that it does: that the influence of forest-cover tends toward equability of rainfall. Such are the tentative conclusions of Mr. Raphael Zon, of the United States Forest Service, the most eminent American authority on the subject. It is the opinion of a number of

foresters and meteorologists that if investigation were extended far enough, the tentative working hypothesis
formulated by Mr. Zon would be established.

Our civil engineer in charge of controlling the flow of
the Mississippi River might be one of those who believed
in this hypothesis: if so, would he be warranted in delay-
ing his project (of control by reservoirs) until Mr. Zon's
hypothesis was established and then acted on? That
would be like waiting for the millennium or (to quote the
vernacular) "until hell freezes over." It might well take a
generation to establish the hypothesis and then a full
century to establish the required areas of forest. The reservoir project could be launched in a decade. The ultimate
source of river-flow lies, of course, in rainfall; but the
immediate source of river-flow, and the source which now
we can control, lies in the streams which constitute the
headwaters of the river's system. Some day, perhaps, man
will be enabled to control the rainfall itself the world over,
but today he knows he can control the headwater streams
region by region. The engineer who controls the headwater streams within a region is working with the most
fundamental source of river control within the range at
present of the art of engineering.

The control of America's population is quite as deep-
seated probably as the control of America's floods and
rivers. America's flow of population is part of the world
flow of population. The ultimate source of population flow
within any region in America lies in the flow of population
the world over, but the immediate source of the region's
population-flow lies in the various communities distributed
throughout the country. The flow of population issues
from these communities—especially from the larger com-

munities. The regulation of this flow is the immediate problem of the regional planner: he deals with the problem of controlling *not the total quantity* of people within a region, but *the distribution* of the quantity which is already there. The regional planner makes no attempt to control the flow of population into his region from other portions of the world; no more than the engineer attempts to control the flow of water into his river basin coming through rainfall from other portions of the world. The regional planner and the engineer, each within his region or his river basin, accepts a given amount or quantity of flow, and then distributes it according to some plan. Each one works with the immediate source of flow and not with the ultimate source. The civil engineer works not to control the world's rainfall, and the regional planner works not to control the rate of world population.

Each of these technicians works within the present range of his particular technique. The physician may be able in time to control the rate of world population and thereby to extend the range and influence of regional planning and of every other social service; indeed, the Western European countries have all made a distinct advance in this direction; but the regional planner who in the meantime guides the flow of population issuing from the communities within his particular region will, like the engineer, be "working at the sources" within his present range.

Again we maintain that the control of any kind of "flow"—whether of water or of population—must take place at the sources of the "stream" rather than at its "mouths." This applies alike to the civil engineer and to the regional planner, but it applies only to the sources which lie within their particular art or technique. It does not apply to the sources which lie beyond and outside of such art or technique. The relation between the world-wide flow of water known as "rainfall" and the local flow within a single river system is similar to the relation between the world-wide "flow" of population and the "flow" within any single region. The relation in each case is between a general and a local flow. Control of the general flow is more fundamental, of course, than control of a local flow. But an effective local control, though not complete, should not be forsaken for the pursuit of a promised general control: the latter pursuit should be carried on and the art of man thus widened, but an art already developed should be utilized to the full measure of its range. Control of the world's rainfall and control of the world's birth rate should both be studied, but not to the neglect of developing the known possibilities of civil engineering and of regional planning.

We are now ready for a more concrete charting and revelation than we have made heretofore of the indigenous and the metropolitan molds.

Chapter XI

REGIONAL CITY VS. METROPOLIS

In order to render as concrete as possible our charting of the indigenous and metropolitan molds, we shall consider, in our general region of New England, a typical locality—an area having the size of an average county, and tributary to a central county seat representative of a large-sized manufacturing town. In order to reveal here principles and tendencies rather than facts and details, we shall picture a fictitious locality rather than an actual one—a locality, however, which is typical of actual conditions. Our central town (or city) we shall assume to have a population of 40,000, and our locality to consist of the territory tributary to this town, embraced within a radius of twenty miles. Radiating from the central city are eight main motor highways, running north, south, east, west, and through each of the four quadrants in between. A rural population of 4,000 is included within twenty rural villages which are located at even intervals throughout the whole locality. The average population within and around each village, therefore, consists of 200 persons, these being contained, we shall assume, in forty domiciles. This distribution of the population is typical roughly of the State of Massachusetts outside of Greater Boston (as shown by the 1920 Census), except that the urban and rural centers are much more sharply defined in our assumed locality than they are under actual conditions.

During the last generation (since 1900)—or, more specifically, between 1900 and 1920—the rural population of Massachusetts, for example, decreased by about 19 per cent., while the urban population (outside of Greater Boston) increased by 43 per cent. We shall assume that the population of our locality is going to increase during the next generation by 43 per cent. The present assumed population of the locality is 44,000 (40,000 in the central city and 4,000 in the surrounding villages): an increase of 43 per cent. would bring the total population to 63,000.

The above description and statistics apply, we will say, to the *present condition* of our fictitious locality. Let us now visualize two possible *future conditions* for this locality. Let us first picture the locality as one destined to constitute a metropolitan mold, and then picture it as a locality destined to constitute an indigenous mold. Specifically, that is, we shall visualize two distinct forms of distribution of the total future population of the locality (the 63,000 souls).

The first picture may be briefly put. It is merely a picture of the metropolitan invasion applied to our fictitious locality. This invasion would take its start from the central community. Its movements here as elsewhere we may liken to a glacier. It is spreading, unthinking, ruthless. Its substance consists of tenements, bungalows, stores, factories, billboards, filling-stations, eating-stands, and other structures whose individual hideousness and collective haphazardness present that unmistakable environment which we call the "slum." Not the slum of poverty, but the slum of commerce. This substance, conceived as a projecting, crawling glacial flow, makes its journey along each of the radiating highways. The twenty rural villages of our locality are penetrated one by one. They are welded together into a common suburban mass without form or articulation; the integrity of each former village (each former human unit) is ironed away; its local government is merged in general administration; its "personality" evaporates. Beyond the villages, the lines of flow, growing thin and puddly, continue their inroad toward the hinterland. In this wise the 63,000 souls become distributed in one continuous mass of straggling lines emanating from an overgorged center. These souls live all in a single environment: not city, not country, but wilderness—the wilderness not of an integrated, ordered nature, but of a standardized, unordered civilization. We have named this the metropolitan environment.

The second picture involves a somewhat longer story—the visualization of the 63,000 souls distributed within an indigenous mold. We assume that our locality contains, inherently, the ingredients of this mold—in the central city, the twenty villages, and in the intervening hills and lakes, providing respectively the bases for developing the urban, communal, and primeval environments. These three elements together form the indigenous environment. Our 63,000 souls can readily be provided for within the limits of our locality without sacrificing the conditions of this indigenous environment. This is evident from the simple tabulation shown on the next page.

This tabulation affords a rough specification of the "indigenous mold." This mold is illustrated in two stages—a present and a future stage. In the present stage only one-tenth of the population live within the rural area, while in the future stage more than a third would live in the rural area. If the assumptions made for this future stage represent truly the potential conditions, then the indigenous mold is capable of absorbing substantial proportions of the population, not only in the urban areas but in the rural territory as well. And the primeval area would be readily

"DIMENSIONS" OF ASSUMED LOCALITY

Radius	20 miles	
Total area ....1,255 sq. m.		100.0%
Primeval area (mountain range and lakes) .... 157 " "		12.5%
Rural area (fields, woodlots, community centers) ..1,093 " "		87.0%
Urban area (central city) .... 5 " "		0.5%

ASSUMED DISTRIBUTION OF POPULATION IN RURAL AREA

Present Distribution:

Number of villages	20
Population per village	200
Number of houses (or domiciles) in or near each village (assuming five persons in a family)	40
Average area per domicile	875 acres
Radius of territory tributary to each village	4.1 miles
Total population provided for	4,000

Future Distribution:

Number of villages	60
Population per village	385
Number of houses in or near each village	77
Average area per domicile	151 acres
Radius of territory tributary to each village	2.4 miles
Total population provided for 23,000

accessible to the people of the whole locality. Thus all three of the "elemental environments" would be provided for within the locality: indeed, the locality would *consist of* these environments. That the assumptions made for the future of our locality do truly represent the potential conditions seems probable in view of the development during the past generation of two modern inventions which affect profoundly the distribution of the population.

One of these developments is the electrical transmission of mechanical power; the other is motor transportation.

"The lengthening of the power belt" is the striking way in which Mr. Philip P. Wells describes the significance of electrical transmission by wire. The factory need not go to Niagara, Niagara can go to the factory: that is, within a radius of some three hundred miles. Coal no longer need be hauled laboriously in freight cars over hundreds of miles of track (requiring more coal to haul it); its latent power, transformed into electric fluid at the pit-head, can be shot through a slender wire to the remotest hamlet. And the future factory can be a smokeless factory. The farmer's son who aspires to be a mechanic need not go to the city in search of a lathe; the lathe can come to him at the end of a three-hundred-mile wire. I say that the lathe "can" come—such is at present the mechanical possibility: it follows, physically speaking, that the farmer's son "need" not go to the city.

Motor transportation is the complement of electrical transmission: through the motor truck the smokeless factory of the rural hamlet can be provided with transportation facilities. But of equal significance to the motor as a carrier of freight is its function as a carrier of passengers. The motor bus is a substitute for the subway. The lawyer's son (or daughter) who aspires to a legal career need not go and live in a large city nor in the suburbs of a large city; he (or she) is enabled, physically, to live in the real country—by private motor or community bus to be in the office promptly in the morning and back again in the village in plenty of time for supper. This more pleasing form of "commuting" is already under way to and from the smaller-sized cities in such areas as our assumed locality represents.

Thus by means of the electric wire and the motor vehicle the job can go to the rural dweller or the rural dweller go to the job, and thus it would seem that the indigenous mold, revealed in severe pattern in the figures above tabulated, represents a distribution of the population which physically *can be*. The indigenous mold has been thus portrayed, in its essence and nakedness, in order to make a concrete picture of it as a physical possibility. In no actual case, of course, would the territory tributary to an urban center constitute a locality of the cut-and-dried character designated in our assumed pattern. But even a little consideration of this pattern should bring out some fundamental points with respect to the planning and revelation of the indigenous American environment. This pattern is no invention of mine nor of any other single human brain: it is merely an attempt at the restoration, and extension through modern instrumentalities, of the basic scheme of regional development, which arose naturally and spontaneously in the endeavor to adapt a given American setting to certain fundamental human desires. The indigenous mold, as revealed in our pattern, seems to meet these desires in specific ways: it is not only something which is physically possible, but something which appears to be basically and psychologically desirable.

The indigenous mold seems to be fundamentally desirable for the reasons which we have previously cited—that it provides for certain fundamental human contacts, viz.:

The contact of man and nature, as provided in the primeval setting.

The generalized contact of man and man, as provided in the rural village community.

The specialized contact of man and man, as provided in the urban and cosmopolitan groupings.

All three of these contacts are specifically provided for in the design of our assumed locality. The primeval setting can be developed and made accessible along the neighboring mountain ranges and around the shores of the various lakes. The village community life can be developed in the numerous rural villages. The residents of each village form a separate "community group" whose common interest consists in the united comprehension of the particular region of the earth in which they dwell and of the little symmetric world of all-round living indigenous to such region. The common interest of the "urban or cosmopolitan group" consists in the comprehension not of any particular region but of some particular field of world-activity—science, art, literature, economics, what you will. These various urban groups can be developed not alone in the central city of our locality, but also *in the sum total of the surrounding villages.*

The assumed total future population of our locality is 63,000; 1,000 of this number might be interested in some particular field of world-activity: these 1,000 people, though they were scattered throughout the villages, could still be formed as a "cosmopolitan group," and the mechanical problem of getting them together for conference and contact would be similar to that of getting together a like group scattered over any other wide area—such as Greater New York. This would be a matter (as now in New York) either of occasionally "staying in town" or of getting together in one of the outskirts. But the "outskirts" would consist of a village instead of a suburb, and transportation would be by motor instead of by subway. The term "regional city" has been applied to this conception of a grouping of villages or small cities within an area, for it combines the attributes of the natural region and the true city: it provides all three elements of the indigenous environment and dissipates the congealed massings which form the substance of the metropolitan environment.

The indigenous development of our assumed locality has been visioned as taking place around a single central city, for the reason that in the typical American locality there are likely to be one or more communities which in one way or another dominate the smaller communities surrounding them. But this condition is accidental and has resulted from the general planlessness accompanying thus far the development of the country. It is no part of the conception of the regional city. This conception is one of a series of community units whose totality constitutes a greater unit. This is illustrated in Oxford, England, where twenty-three near-independent college units constitute the greater unit of the University. The various units should shine not by the reflected light from a central star but each by its own light as a member of an "all-star cast." The combination of communities forming a regional city should form a regional symphony in which each member, whether in the industrial or the cultural field, should develop itself as an instrument of excellence in some specialty of the arts of a true civilization. In short, the regional city is a giant orchestration of varied life (urban, communal, and even primeval) as against the dull cacophony of standardized existence presented by the modern metropolis.

The regional city is a concrete conception of the indigenous mold as the metropolis is of the metropolitan mold. This conception is presented in its full nakedness and angularity, not as a suggested pattern toward which necessarily to work in a given development, but as a concrete precipitant to clarify our ideas regarding a complex and confusing subject. Our particular problem in regional planning (and in the New Exploration) deals with the distribution of a given population within a region. Our particular goal is to guide the flow of population into some form of the indigenous mold (the environment of real living) and to deter it from any form of the metropolitan mold (the environment of mere existence). This goal presents a double task: one task consists in establishing that portion of environment which we have called the *setting;* the other consists in developing that portion called *activity.* These two tasks we shall consider in the next two chapters. One relates concretely to the location of barriers for coping with the metropolitan invasion; the other relates to bringing forth the full potentiality of the indigenous environment. One is a physical problem, the other is a psychologic problem: one is a matter of comprehensive engineering, the other of synthetic art.

Chapter XII

CONTROLLING THE METROPOLITAN INVASION

"Regional planning," as Mr. Walter Prichard Eaton said at a recent planning conference, "is a hand on the rudder of evolution. It is an acid test of how far we are the captains of our fate."

How far we are such "captains" depends upon our vision; upon our powers of revelation; upon our ability to see ourselves in the perspective of evolution and within the plans of nature. The plans of physical nature might be put into two great classes—those which are permanent and inherent, and those which are temporary and (of a sort) cataclysmic. Plans of the first class may be called *indigenous;* those of the second class, *intrusive.* An example is at hand in the invasion by the ice-sheet of the original landscape (and the ultimate landscape) of New England and North America. While the glacier was here it must have seemed to be the main plan—it was dynamic and devastating; but it proved to be only an interruption. It was the indigenous and not the intrusive landscape which was to endure: the original "plan" became the ultimate one, and what appeared to belong merely to the past turned out to belong to the future—and to the ages.

As with geology, so perhaps with certain human processes taking place upon the map of New England and of America. The Atlantic Plain from Maine to Georgia is possessed (in past and future) of a certain indigenous character and mold which seems destined to spread throughout America. It is a growing and not a static thing. It is based on the cultures of the past—British, Continental, and others. The fulfillment of these cultures requires modern mechanical processes to free its energies from the absorption of mechanical routine. If we would be cultured beings and not beasts, then the steamship should replace the Roman galley and its slaves. But the steamship in the hands of the Romans—or of the Roman attitude—would result in more slaves rather than fewer. Where mechanics run faster than culture, the latter is the loser. A sudden jump in mechanical ingenuity, therefore, with its attendant industrial and metropolitan development, must tend to cut in on a plodding orderly development of culture: it must act to some extent as an "intrusive" upon such culture. Through such developments as the railroad in the sixties, and motor transportation and electric transmission of power, since the nineties, a series of sudden jumps has taken place in this country. The leisurely growth of an American indigenous culture, which promised so much before the Civil War, has been burked, or diverted into purely metropolitan interests and concerns.

This metropolitan invasion is, I believe, in the nature of an interruption, but whether it will amount actually to this or to our permanent undoing depends on what we are going to do about it. The attitude of the regional planner, as conceived in this particular Philosophy of Regional Planning, is to view this phenomenon as an interruption, to cope with it as a distinct intruder, and to proceed with the development of the indigenous America as something belonging to the future as well as to the past. The coming of the metropolitan invasion, overnight as it were, like a flood suddenly set loose from a thousand ruptured reservoirs, may be viewed as the emergent reason, the *occasion* if you please, for the dormant but awakening movement of regional planning and the New Exploration.

The "thousand ruptured reservoirs" refer to the great metropolitan centers (or the thousand and one centers large and small) which are scattered throughout the country. For every city, every metropolitan center, is a source of flow as well as a mouth thereof. The city is the mouth for commodity-flow, but it is the source of population-flow. The city, or more precisely the metropolis, we have compared to a mill-pond from which the "backflow of population" penetrates the hinterland. The metropolis we have compared also to a lake which overflows its normal banks; and in this sense it is a ruptured reservoir. It may be large or small: New York is such a reservoir, and so is Blanktown, Pennsylvania. From each the "flood waters" of metropolitanism have broken away.

The flow of metropolitanism we have compared loosely with the flow of waters—but we must now be more precise: we must compare it with the flow of *flood waters*. Metropolitan development is the result of revolution—the industrial revolution. It has come upon us, in its potent form, within a generation. And its potence lies not so much in the particular thing it is as in the *suddenness* of its appearance. This fact is critical: it is critical as to our choice of means for coping with the general problem. One set of means is required for controlling the general normal flow issuing from the upland headwaters; but a different set of means is needed for handling the flow issuing from an upland reservoir which has suddenly broken down.

There are two chief means for controlling the normal

flow of a river—such as the Mississippi. One consists in a series of storage reservoirs located in the regions of the upland headwaters. The other consists in a series of barriers located in and along the river throughout its lower stretches. These barriers consist either of dams—embankments laid across the stream for actually retarding the waters; or else of levees—embankments laid parallel to the stream for holding the waters intact. Both of these means (the reservoirs upstream and the embankments downstream) may be required to control a river's flow; and even then, of course, the stream may get out of bounds. If now the upland reservoir breaks down, then the full strain comes on the downstream embankments. And if in the first place the reservoir was never built, then all the more need of the downstream embankments. The building of embankments downstream will not always make up for neglect in the proper building of reservoirs upstream. But if the reservoirs simply are not there, or if, being there, they break down, then we must pin our faith to the dams and the levees in case of a sudden deluge: these embankments in a case like this are in the nature of emergency breastworks.

Some such situation as this confronts us in our problem of controlling the flow of population and of metropolitanism. The center of population, whether city or metropolis, is the "reservoir." If it be a true city, with definite boundaries and an individual integrity, then it forms a "reservoir" which is properly constructed: it will not leak nor break down; if it grows in population, its limits may expand, but its integrity will be preserved; if a portion of its population migrates, it can be absorbed in some neighboring (and properly constructed) "reservoir." Cities of this kind would have to be controlled and planned. Letchworth and Welwyn in England are cities of this kind.

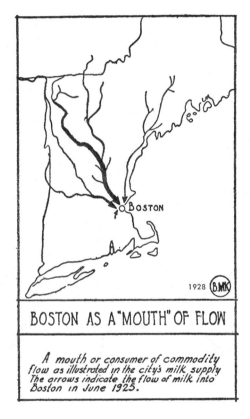

BOSTON AS A "MOUTH" OF FLOW

A mouth or consumer of commodity flow as illustrated in the city's milk supply. The arrows indicate the flow of milk into Boston in June 1925.

These and the other so-called "garden cities," in England and on the Continent, have been planned and built upon a preconceived idea—part of which is to hold a population within bounds as a definite unit or reservoir of human society. Cities of this type are being established in America. One of the most recent projects of the sort is the

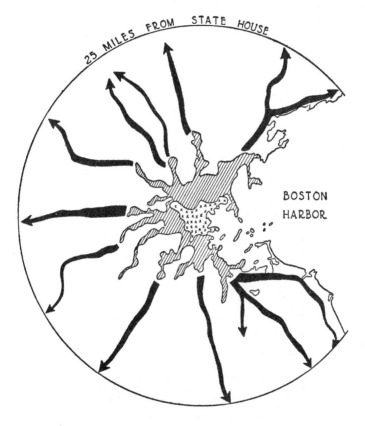

25 MILES FROM STATE HOUSE

BOSTON
HARBOR

LEGEND

Population increase less than 10 %
Population increase from 10 to 80%
Present trend of population flow

1928

BOSTON AS A "SOURCE" OF FLOW

A source or reservoir of metropolitan
flow as illustrated in the backflow of population 1910 to 1925.

planned city of Radburn, which is being built near Pater-
son, New Jersey, by the City Housing Corporation.

If on the other hand the center of population is not a
city but a metropolis (whether large or small), then it
forms a "reservoir" which is *not* properly constructed.
New York is the outstanding example of a broken-down
reservoir of population. The typical center of population
in this country is a metropolis—a leaky or ruptured reservoir, whether New York or Blanktown, Pennsylvania.
From each such center is issuing a deluge of metropolitanism. What manner of embankments (what "dams" and
what "levees") can we construct "downstream" to hold in
check this deluge?

But first of all, what is "downstream" and what is "upstream"? Let us seek the answer in some actual region—
take the Connecticut River valley in New England.

Two sets of streams are flowing in the Connecticut
River valley—one set is flowing south and the other north;
one set is flowing down the valley and the other up the
valley. Streams of water are flowing southward down the
valley, and streams of population are flowing northward
up the valley. The sources of one set of streams lie in the
headwaters of the river's basin—the White Mountains,
the Green Mountains, the Berkshires, and elsewhere: the
main sources of the other set lie in the big cities located
at the lower end of the valley—in Springfield, in Hartford,
and in the other centers southward to Long Island Sound.
A main stream of water (the Connecticut River) flows
southward and downward: a main stream of metropolitanism flows northward and upward along the selfsame
Connecticut River. What is downstream for one stream
is upstream for the other. And so in this case the deluge

of population and of metropolitanism appears to flow "up-hill": "upstream" lies among the big cities and towns in the region of Long Island Sound, while "downstream" lies in the upper valley regions of New Hampshire and Vermont.

This case is typical. It applies at least to the whole Atlantic Plain from Maine to Georgia where a third of the Nation's population dwells. The streams of water on this plain flow, generally speaking, southward and eastward from the Appalachian Mountain barrier into the Atlantic Ocean, while the streams of metropolitanism flow northward and westward (and upward) from the Atlantic seaboard toward the Appalachian barrier. Hence "upstream" is on the Atlantic seaboard, while "downstream" is on the Appalachian barrier.

New England illustrates this fact. The main streams of water flow south and east from the main divide—the Penobscot, Kennebec, Androscoggin, Saco, Merrimac, Thames, Connecticut, and Housatonic. The streams of metropolitanism follow the main lines of traffic up these very rivers from the seaboard—from Bangor, Portland, Portsmouth, Boston, New London, New Haven, and Bridgeport. There are, of course, modifications to this general rule. From Boston, the dominant metropolis of New England, the lines of traffic and development radiate in almost all directions, and so the main streams of our "deluge" cross one another at various angles.

As with Boston, so with the lesser metropolises—Worcester and Springfield and Fitchburg and the rest. In each case streams of metropolitan development tend to flow along the main lines of traffic radiating from the particular center and "source." Hence "upstream" in each

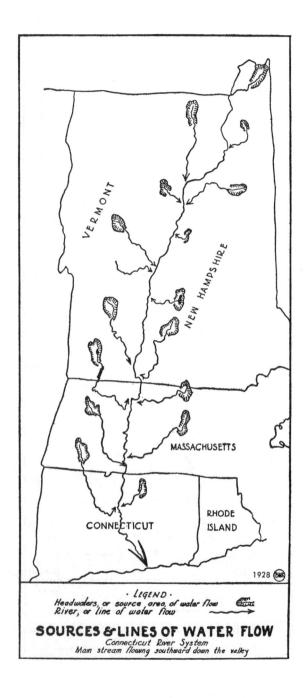

· LEGEND ·
Headwaters, or source area, of water flow
River, or line of water flow

SOURCES & LINES OF WATER FLOW
Connecticut River System
Main stream flowing southward down the valley

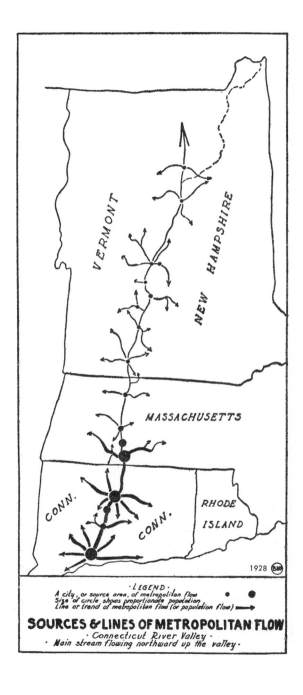

· LEGEND ·
A city, or source area, of metropolitan flow
Size of circle shows proportionate population
Line or trend of metropolitan flow (or population flow)

SOURCES & LINES OF METROPOLITAN FLOW
· Connecticut River Valley ·
· Main stream flowing northward up the valley ·

case is at the *center,* while "downstream" is *outward* along each main highway.

Let us return to our former question: What manner of embankments (what "dams" and what "levees") can we construct "downstream" to hold our deluge in check? Let us take a simple case—the deluge flowing from a small metropolis into the surrounding tributary area. Again we shall assume the existence of a fictitious locality. Another diagrammatic pattern. Assume a locality similar to that described in our last chapter: a circular area of twenty-mile radius, containing a central metropolis of 40,000 population and a number of small villages in even distribution. Four main highways (not eight) extend outward from the central town—north, south, east, and west. Side roads cross the main roads at regular intervals. The periphery of the locality consists of a range of hills and low mountains from which four ridges extend in toward the central town through the middle of each quadrant (northwest, northeast, etc.).

If left alone, the metropolitan deluge will flow out along the main highways (and the side highways) in the fashion described in the last chapter, distributing the population in a series of continuous strings, which together would make a metropolitan cobweb of the locality. In this way the area with its several villages would become engulfed by the metropolitan flood. What are the barriers and footholds supplied by nature in this locality for narrowing and checking the full workings of this cataclysm? What topographic features are there, and what common public ground, which could be developed as a series of "embankments"?

The outstanding topographic feature consists of the range of hills and mountains encircling the locality, together with the four ridges reaching toward the central city. This could be reserved as a common public ground, serving the double purpose of a public forest and a public playground. It might be called a "wilderness area." It would form a linear area, or belt, around and through the locality, well adapted for camping and primitive travel (by foot or horseback). Overnight, week-end, and vacation trips could be made from the central city and from the adjacent villages by way of a number of varied circuits. This series of open areas and ways would form a distinct realm: it would be a primeval realm (or near-primeval)—the opposite realm from the metropolitan. These open ways (along the crestlines) mark the lines for developing the primeval environment, while the motor ways mark the lines for extending the metropolitan environment. The motor ways form the channels of the metropolitan flood, while the open ways (crossing and flanking the motor ways) form "dams" and "levees" for controlling the flood. Where the motor way crosses the open way, the traffic of course would be allowed to pass; but traffic is one thing, and roadside development is quite another thing. The highway is for traffic and for travel, not (of necessity) for industry or residence. The open way across the motor way would form a barrier not to traffic but to metropolitan development: it would be a "dam" across the path of the metropolitan flood.

A system of open ways of this design would form a series of breaks in the metropolitan deluge: it would divide—or tend to divide—the flood waters of metropolitanism into separate "basins" and thereby tend to avert their com-

plete and total confluence. This it would do in two ways
—physically and psychologically. Wayside structures
within the crossing of an open way would be eliminated,
or else they would be established under public regulation
in accordance with some plan. But quite as important perhaps as this physical control would be the opportunity
provided by the open way for carrying out in practical
fashion the latent if not evident desire, within a large body
of the people, for experiencing the opposite mode of life
from that provided for by the channels of metropolitan
civilization. The motor way marks a belt of travel devoted
to establishing a certain phase of civilization: the open
way reveals a belt of travel dedicated to the development
of a counter phase of civilization. One opens a channel for
the expansion of the "material fact": the other opens a
trail for the growth of the "spiritual form." The open way,
practically equipped with facilities for camping and for
walking or leisurely conveyance, provides definitely for
the exercise, and hence for the increased strength, of those
cultural powers within human society which would develop
the country for the innate ultimate purposes of true *living*
and not merely for the routine of mechanical *existence*.
In this way we would stimulate within the individual an
inner and immediate desire for controlling an over-me-
chanical civilization—something more potent perhaps
than the control alone by outward physical means.

With this point in mind, it looks as if the "levee" would
be quite as important as the "dam." The open way flanking the motor way, even at a remote distance, if equipped
for actual use as a zone of primeval sojourn and outdoor
living, might form in the public consciousness a forbidding of the metropolitan flood which would be quite as ef-

fective as the occasional physical barrier across the flood's path. "Yes," perhaps you say, "both notions—the forbidding and the barrier—are equally weak." Maybe so. Maybe we are doomed to be engulfed. But here is a means at our disposal—sticking out of the countryside and its topography. It is a means which will prove weak or strong according as you and I—as engineers, as citizens—prove weak or strong.

Here, then, is one line of strategy for coping with the metropolitan flood—a slender thread perhaps, but something that nature still holds out to us. It is the utilization of the natural open ways which still remain. Take Massachusetts. There is the open way provided by the crestline of the Berkshires, southward from Hoosac Mountain; there is in contrast the way provided by the meandering Ipswich River which skirts the Boston Basin, and by the Concord River, and by other rivers with their bordering swamps and wooded bottomlands; there is the long, deep canyon of the Deerfield River in the western counties, flanking the Mohawk Highway on either side; there is the long, winding belt of "pine barrens" along the backbone of Cape Cod; there are other lines of primeval, or near-primeval, travel interwoven with the metropolitan on the map of Massachusetts. These definite lines of open lands between the towns and villages—these wild lands, and near-wild lands, and wastelands—form together the ingredients of a system. It is a system crossing, flanking, and interlocking with another system—that, namely, of the motor ways and the lines of metropolitan flow radiating from Boston and from the several lesser metropolises throughout the State. Numberless walking-circuits are provided by these open ways around and about the various cities and towns. Here is a potential system of "levees" as if designed by nature to fit a man-made system. Here is a latent strategy for controlling, in part at least, the metropolitan invasion.

Let us return to our diagrammatic locality. Let us assume that the strategy just outlined has succeeded within our assumed locality and that the mountain open ways have prevented a general confluence of the metropolitan flood and have segregated it into four separate basins. How shall the flood be controlled within each basin? Here is a matter which requires a further strategy—something to complete and complement the system of "levees" above described.

This further complemental strategy consists of another system of levees. This system is an adjunct of the motor way system: it consists of a series of open ways, or zones, straddling the motor road between successive towns or villages. The object within each such wayside zone between two towns is to keep the abutting land, on both sides of the highway, free from all structures and uses of land except those appropriate to an intertown development. A zone section of this kind may be called an "intertown."

The *intertown* is in the nature of a double levee inclosing the channel itself of the traffic stream. Through this levee the flow of traffic would of course be allowed to pass, but not the flow of metropolitanism. The motor truck is one thing, while the factory is quite another: the family sedan is one thing, while the apartment house is something else. The town (the real town, large or small) is the natural home of homes: it is the unit of human society; it is an evolution from the camp fire and the wig-

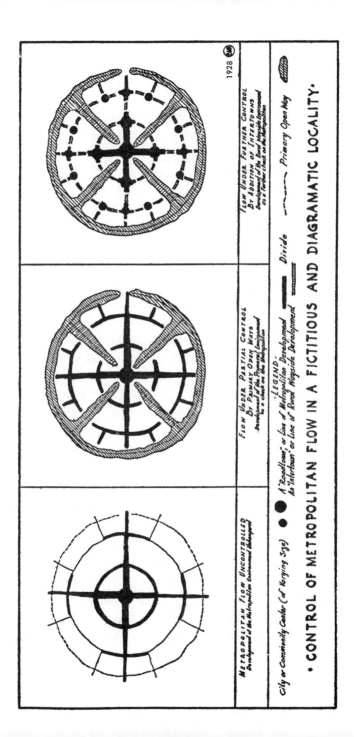

1928

METROPOLITAN FLOW UNCONTROLLED
Development of the Metropolitan Environment Undeveloped

FLOW UNDER PARTIAL CONTROL
BY PRIMARY OPEN WAYS
Development of the Primary Lineipment
as a check on the Metropolitan

FLOW UNDER FURTHER CONTROL
BY ADDITION OF INTERTOWNS
Development of the Rural Wayside Environment
as a further check on the Metropolitan

·LEGEND·

City or Community Center (of Varying Size)   ●   A 'Roadtown'; or Line of Metropolitan Development ——— Divide ——— Primary Open Way ⬭
An 'Intertown' or Line of Rural Wayside Development

· CONTROL OF METROPOLITAN FLOW IN A FICTITIOUS AND DIAGRAMATIC LOCALITY·

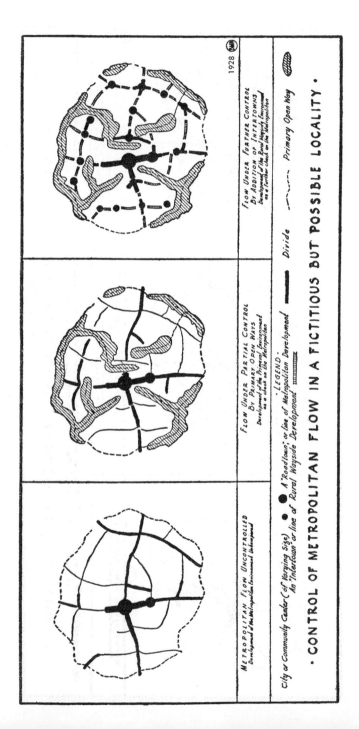

1928

METROPOLITAN FLOW UNCONTROLLED
Development of the Metropolitan Environment Unhampered

FLOW UNDER PARTIAL CONTROL
BY PRIMARY OPEN WAYS
*Development of the Primeval Environment
as a check on the Metropolitan*

FLOW UNDER FURTHER CONTROL
BY ADDITION OF INTERTOWNS
*Development of the Rural Wayside Environment
as a further check on the Metropolitan*

· LEGEND ·

● City or Community Center (of Varying Size)   ● A "Roadtown" or line of Metropolitan Development   ━━━ Divide   ┈┈┈ Primary Open Way

● An "Intertown" or line of Rural Wayside Development ┉┉┉┉

· CONTROL OF METROPOLITAN FLOW IN A FICTITIOUS BUT POSSIBLE LOCALITY ·

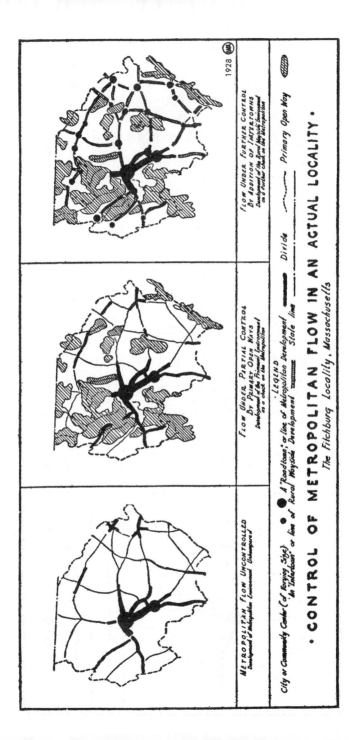

1928

METROPOLITAN FLOW UNCONTROLLED
Development of Metropolitan Commercial Undampered

FLOW UNDER PARTIAL CONTROL
BY PRIMARY OPEN WAYS
Development of the Primary Open Way lines
as a check on the Metropolitan

FLOW UNDER FURTHER CONTROL
BY ADDITION OF INTER-TOWNS
Development of the Rural Wayside Development
as a further check on the Metropolitan

LEGEND

City or Community Center (of Varying Size) An "Intertown" or line of Rural Wayside Development ● A "Roadtown" or line of Metropolitan Development Divide ━━━ State line ▭▭▭ Primary Open Way ▨▨▨

· CONTROL OF METROPOLITAN FLOW IN AN ACTUAL LOCALITY ·
The Fitchburg Locality, Massachusetts

wam village; it is the natural and the efficient seat of human residence and industry. The intertown is the natural home of the "passing stream of traffic"—and of travelers: it is the link *between* the units of society; it is a humanly directed evolution of the "open road"—of the sphere which belongs to no unit of society but to all humanity. The town belongs to itself—to its own community: the intertown belongs to the region—and the State. The intertown is a breathing-valve in the geographic body-politic.

The alternative to the intertown is the "roadtown"—a continuous tunnel of structures from one end of the State to the other. Under this condition most of us would never be able to get out of town at all: for most of us the countryside would vanish from our sight; our patriotism would emanate not from our "woods and templed hills" but from our wayside shacks and tenements. "Roadtown" is the embodiment of the metropolitan flood—it is the flood itself: it is an outshoot of the wilderness of civilization. The intertown would supplant this wilderness. But do not fear. It would *not* supplant it by the wilderness of nature.

The intertown is not of necessity a belt of unpeopled country—it is not necessarily a park or a wooded canopy: it may be such in places, but on the whole it is merely a zone or area in which the "flood" must not run wild. The intertown is no attempt to rid the road of houses. It is not possible, nor is it desirable, to attempt in any wholesale fashion to "put the town off the street." Fear not, we have no notion of sounding a civic curfew. Structures of every conceivable kind there must always be to decorate the wayside. But let us see that they do in truth *decorate!* The structural ingredients of an ordered civilization and of a wilderness of civilization are the same: they are factories and stores and residences and a host of other buildings and plants. So are the ingredients of a salad and of a garbage pile the same. The ingredients in one case are assembled, while in the other case they are "chucked together." The various parts of a true town—and of a true intertown—are assembled in accordance with some idea, but in the metropolis and in the "roadtown" the parts are merely chucked together. There is no need of this "chucking" process: under proper regulation the parts can be assembled. That is the function of planning. And the intertown should be planned, as well as the town.

What are the "structural ingredients" which, whether we like it or not, do in fact form the present typical wayside development—the ingredients with which we should have to deal, one way or another, in the planning of an intertown? The structures referred to may be placed in three classes:

First: *Advertising structures*—billboards of varying degree.

Elsewhere I have made my comments upon this subject, and so here I shall simply quote: [1]

These [advertising structures] may be viewed from two angles—the public's and the advertiser's. The public does not really need them: people can find out what to buy through other advertising media. The wayside signs which interest the public are those which affect the public and not the individual. "Greenfield 40 miles," "Sharp Curve," "Stop Forest Fires"—these signs affect the whole of us. "Stop That Cough," "Use a Green Lip Stick!"—these can interest only coughers and self-

[1] "To Keep Malignant Growths Off Our Highways." *Boston Evening Transcript,* Feb. 21, 1928.

adorners. The advertiser is of course interested in billboards. But he is interested only because his rival is. Each one forces the other one to it; it is merely a matter of "keeping up with the Jones's," as with the world's great navies. Britain and America long ago declared a disarmament within a certain realm, namely the Great Lakes. This saves both nations a whole lot of money. The advertisers could do likewise with their implements of warfare—they could declare a "disarmament" within a certain realm, that, namely, of the Wayside Billboard. This would also save a whole lot of money. It would remove a non-utility from the roadside and a flagrant blinder from the countryside. The billboard needs no regulation and no planning—all it needs is abolition.

Both the eating-place and the filling-station are distributed almost wholly according to the chance game which goes with unregulated industry in general. There is a superfluity of eating-stands and an injudicious mixture of filling-stations; if there be design in the distribution of the latter by one company, the effect is too often offset by the independent design of a rival company.

Second: *Intertown utilities*—those required at frequent intervals or desirable at appropriate sites: inns and eating-establishments; outlook towers, gift shops, and entertainment quarters; garages and filling-stations.

The outstanding intertown utilities consist of the eating-place and the filling-station. These present a double problem: that of distributing them at proper intervals along the road; and that of selecting an architecture in keeping with their setting.

Architecturally the stations, whether for eating or filling, are of the stark pattern which has made them universally notorious. This need not be. A little skilled attention directed toward gasoline tanks, garages, and toward merchant plants in general, would do for the structure as a whole what a sense of art has already done for the store window on our city streets. There is nothing more inadequate architecturally than the average wayside "eating-joint," while there is nothing more pleasant and hospitable than the cozy dining-room (whether inn, tea house, or cabin) which is fitted into the setting of some wayside natural feature or historic background—be it mountain vista or mill-pond.

The problem of intertown utilities, therefore, is one of choosing proper intervals and of using our powers of art. Here is something which does need regulation and planning; and the start is being made in our various State zoning laws.

Third: *Town structures*—those normally constituting the town unit: residences of various types; churches, school houses, and other public buildings; theaters, baseball grounds, and other recreative structures; stores and office buildings; factories and other industrial plants.

The outstanding town structures which find their way into the intertown areas consist for the most part of residences and stores. Bungalows of typical mushroom architecture and tenements of a few ungainly designs are shuffled along the wayside, while the blatant chain store is huddled with its kind in various random groups. Here again one of the problems is the selecting of an architecture, for the several types of buildings, which will be in keeping with the varying natural settings.

But aside from this matter of appearances there is the other problem of distribution. Town structures properly belong in town. But very often people want to live out in the open country—not in a little village but away off by themselves. Farmhouses almost of necessity are located far apart. Provision should certainly be made for this form of rural environment. Segregated establishments of this kind, whether for farming or for purely residential purposes, should (and do) take up their place along the main highways. Their presence thus in segregated fashion does not impair at all the essential character of the intertown. In no wise can a farmhouse here and there, or an estate, or a fitting residence, be considered a part of the metropolitan flood—or slum. But where such plants become too thick and extend unduly from their village base, then, however good the aspect and the architecture, each place and home has lost the very isolation sought; "roadtown" has seized the open way; and the metropolitan invasion, however elegantly dressed, has captured a portion of our common countryside. Here is another matter which requires regulation—and the most careful kind of planning.

The intertown belongs to the State: its improvement must result from a State-wide conscience. The application of such a conscience to this matter has taken root apparently in the State of Massachusetts. A proposed law is being considered by the legislature for "zoning the State highways." This would provide for the regulation of structures between the villages (in unzoned townships) on a strip running 500 feet back from each side of the State highway. It would apply especially to advertising structures and to intertown utilities. Regulation of this kind could be supplemented by the purchase of lands along the highways for public reservations—State parks and forests, or town forests dedicated to public use. Such total sphere of public regulation would constitute the intertown. In few cases perhaps could this sphere extend the complete distance from village to village. But wherever a link could be established, whether by zoning or by reservation, a *levee* would be injected into the channel itself of metropolitanism. A series of such levees following the highway system would complement that other system of levees made by the "open ways" which we have previously described.

These two systems of levees constitute a double strategy for controlling the metropolitan invasion. They would, as applied to our assumed locality, completely hold the flood in check: the open ways along the mountain crestlines would hold the "waters" within four separate basins, while the intertowns within each basin would prevent their flow along the channels of traffic. Suppose this strategy to be carried out as the result of a "State-wide" or a "locality" conscience—then would the locality's population have distributed themselves in units and not undifferentiated masses of humanity. The locality would be spared the fate of becoming a metropolis, or a "metropolitan district"; instead the foundation would be laid for its development toward that indigenous mold which we have called the "regional city."

An illustration of this double strategy is at hand in the State of Massachusetts. A plan is being made for establishing both systems of "levees" throughout the State. The details of this plan form too long a story to relate in this book. But the outlines may be very briefly stated. This plan is being made by a quasi-official commission known as the Governor's Committee on the Needs and Uses of

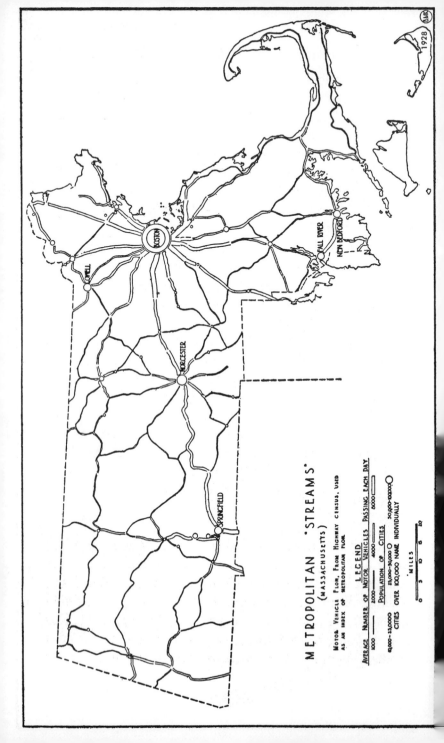

METROPOLITAN "STREAMS"
(MASSACHUSETTS)

MOTOR VEHICLE FLOW, FROM HIGHWAY CENSUS, USED
AS AN INDEX OF METROPOLITAN FLOW.

LEGEND

AVERAGE NUMBER OF MOTOR VEHICLES PASSING EACH DAY
1000 ——— 2000 ——— 4000 ——— 8000 ☰☰☰

POPULATION OF CITIES
10,000-25,000 ○   25,000-50,000 ○   50,000-100,000 ◯
CITIES OVER 100,000 NAME INDIVIDUALLY

MILES
0   5   10   15   20

1928

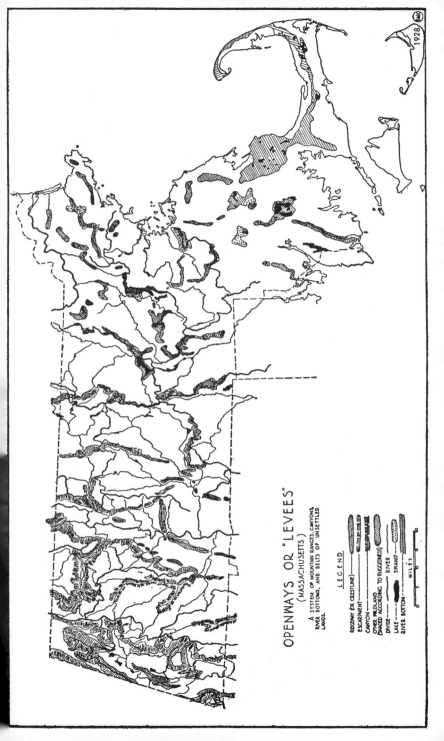

OPENWAYS OR "LEVEES"
(MASSACHUSETTS)

A SYSTEM OF MOUNTAIN RANGES, CANYONS,
RIVER BOTTOMS, AND BELTS OF UNSETTLED
LANDS.

LEGEND

RIDGEWAY (OR CRESTLINE)

ESCARPMENT

CANYON

OTHER WILDLAND
(SHADED ACCORDING TO RUGGEDNESS)

DIVIDE ——— RIVER

LAKE ——— SWAMP

RIVER BOTTOM

MILES

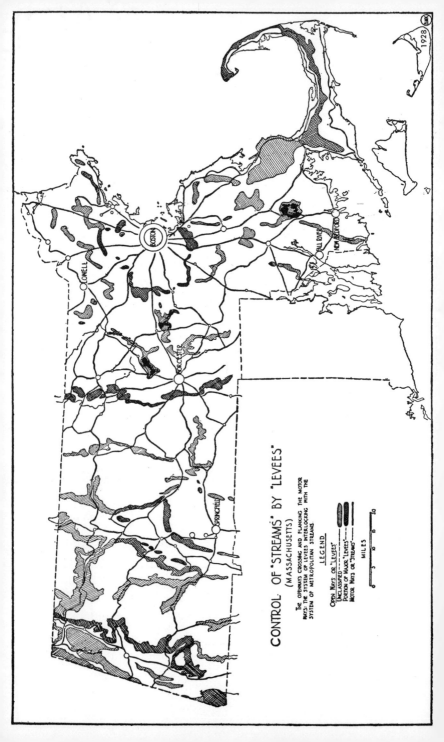

CONTROL OF "STREAMS" BY "LEVEES"
(MASSACHUSETTS)

THE OPENWAYS CROSSING AND FLANKING THE MOTOR
WAYS: THE SYSTEM OF LEVEES INTERLOCKING WITH THE
SYSTEM OF METROPOLITAN STREAMS

LEGEND

OPEN WAYS OR "LEVEES"
UNCLASSIFIED
PORTION OF MAJOR "LEVEES"
MOTOR WAYS OR "STREAMS"

MILES
0   5   10   15   20

Open Spaces.[1] The plan consists of three main chartings, as follows:

1. The main *metropolitan streams* flowing out of Boston and the lesser metropolises (that is, all cities having a population of 10,000 and over). The motor traffic flow (taken from the State highway census) is used, in each section of each motor way, as a measure of the present and forthcoming flow of metropolitan development in such section. This presents a map of the metropolitan flood, or invasion, which is to be controlled.

2. The main topographic features and lanes of unsettled, or undersettled, country which cross and flank the motor ways in such manner as to be suitable for development as *open ways*, or major *"levees,"* for checking or affecting the metropolitan flow. These open ways consist of the following classes:

Mountain crestline and summits (such as the Mt. Holyoke range).

Escarpment, or steep slope from a lowland to an upland (as the west side of Hoosac Mountain).

Canyon, or steep valley along a stream (the Deerfield River).

River Bottom, or level valley along a stream (Ipswich River).

Swamp (the Great Cedar Swamp, and others).

Beach (wherever sufficiently unsettled).

Lake and lake shore (Wachusett Reservoir and others).

Other wild land, or remote land, of miscellaneous topog-

[1] A committee of seventeen members representing the State's chief organizations devoted to outdoor living. Charles S. Bird Jr. of Boston is the chairman.

raphy—a glacial sand plain, an area of glacial hillocks (the Walden Pond locality and elsewhere).

These reservations are of varied legal status: the State park, the State forest, the town forest, the game refuge, the bird sanctuary. Each status represents a special field of outdoor cultural activity: in addition, the public forest (whether State or town) represents a field of industrial development.

Each of these open ways has been charted to meet three tests; namely, that it cross or flank an adjacent motor way (the Hoosac Mountain escarpment crossing the Mohawk highway; the Deerfield River canyon flanking both sides of the same Mohawk highway); that it be sufficiently remote from population centers to constitute a wild or semi-wild area; and that it be sufficiently accessible to population centers to be usable therefrom as a practical route for walking and camping.

This charting presents a map of a system for controlling the metropolitan flow taking place within the counter system formed by the motor ways.

3. Five critical areas, or sections of the designated open ways, selected for initial acquisition and development. Each area is selected in view of its strategic or pivotal location in a major open way or primary "levee." The areas are:

The Hoosac Mountain Escarpment, pivotal in the development of a major levee along the Berkshire ranges and their extensions in Connecticut and by way of the Green Mountains in Vermont.

The Connecticut Valley Highlands, encircling Northampton and Amherst, pivotal in the development of a double levee along the length of the Connecticut River.

The Wachusett-Watatic Ridgeway, near Fitchburg, pivotal section of a major levee across central New England from Rhode Island to the White Mountains of New Hampshire.

The Walden Pond Locality, near Concord, home of Thoreau, pivotal in a projected levee for encircling Greater Boston.

The Barnstable Cross-section, across the town of Barnstable from the ocean to Cape Cod Bay, pivotal in a levee extending throughout Cape Cod and into southeastern Massachusetts.

This charting presents a "war map" of a general strategy of initial action, not only with respect to Massachusetts but to New England. Each of the five areas marks a project for the acquisition of public reservations. Detailed chartings based on field work are being made for one of these projects—the *Wachusett-Watatic Ridgeway.*

This plan of the Governor's Committee on Open Spaces is an illustration of a regional plan of State-wide dimensions. It is a State plan. While not primarily a plan for the conservation of *physical* natural resources, it incidentally provides for conserving the forest resource and thereby the run-off from the upland headwaters of the State's rivers. But its primary purpose is the one of which we have treated in this book—namely, the development of the *psychologic* resource—environment. Its purpose is to develop the indigenous environment—especially the primeval and the wayside rural environments. It is a dynamic and not a static plan: it deals with a force or flow. It deals with a particular flow. This is not the flow of water; it is not the flow of commodities; it is the flow of population and its attendant development; it is the flow of material civilization in its present phase—the metropolitan phase. It sets forth a strategy for coping with this flow—a specific line of action for controlling the metropolitan invasion.

The extension of this plan for the State of Massachusetts would make a plan for the general region of New England. The three chartings cited above can be made for one region as well as another. Indeed this plan for Massachusetts can be taken as a first step in a plan for New England. The main strategy is already laid down for coping with the metropolitan flood throughout New England—the main "levees" are indicated. One of these follows roughly the divide between the Merrimac and Connecticut River basins, from the White Mountains southward toward Rhode Island. A wilderness walking-trail, already projected on this line (and in parts completed), marks the development of a continuous open way. The *Wachusett-Watatic project,* extended into New Hampshire to include the present Wapack project (from Watatic Mountain to Pack Monadnock) marks the initial action toward the completion of this important New England levee. Another levee might follow the two sides of the Connecticut River, and we have the project (around Northampton and Amherst) for initiating this. But the chief levee of all lies along the Green Mountain-Berkshire Range, where the mountain footway of the Long Trail has for several years marked a line of action. The *Hoosac Mountain project,* extended up the Deerfield gorge to Stratton Mountain in Vermont, would bridge the critical portion, in New England, of this backbone of open ways.

For here in this Green Mountain-Berkshire Range we

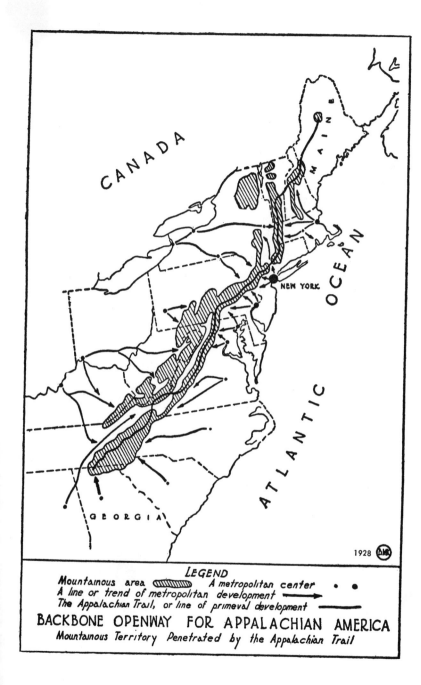

CANADA

MAINE

NEW YORK

ATLANTIC OCEAN

GEORGIA

1928

BACKBONE OPENWAY FOR APPALACHIAN AMERICA
Mountainous Territory Penetrated by the Appalachian Trail

are on the backbone levee of the whole Atlantic border from Canada to Georgia. This levee follows the main mountain way—through the Hudson Highlands, along the Blue Ridge of Pennsylvania and Virginia, and throughout the fastness of the great Carolina Highland. Here is the backbone of Appalachian America. Here is the barrier of barriers within this world-empire of industrial and metropolitan upheaval. We have here already laid, both on the ground and in the public mind, the thread on which to weave this basic barrier. This is the projected mountain footway known as the Appalachian Trail. This Trail is in the making, and in many sections it is made, from Mt. Katahdin, Maine, down to Cohutta Mountain, Georgia. Here is marked the main open way across the metropolitan deluge issuing from the ports of the Atlantic seaboard. This open way, when once it really opens, would form the base throughout eastern populous America for controlling the metropolitan invasion.

Chapter XIII

DEVELOPING THE INDIGENOUS ENVIRONMENT

"Before you can properly remodel a house you must first live in it."

This keen bit of wisdom born of thoughtful experience was handed to me recently by a bright young housewife. She went on to say that actual living in a house was the only way to really know the house and to find out what one really wanted. Using a phrase quoted earlier, she would have said that it was the only way to cross the "woof of reality with the warp of desire." Her comment reiterates the wisdom of Raymond Unwin, already quoted, that the only real way to design a house is first to visualize the actual life, or "activity," which is to take place therein. As with a house, so with the other types of "habitats"— the community, the countryside, or any particular environment—we must live in it, or attempt anyhow the activity of living, before we can design or reveal its innate possibilities. The "players" (all the men and women) must begin their art before the "stage" (all the world) can become a proper setting for the inspired activity which we have called true "living."

Living, according to our definition, consists not in toil nor "decreation" but in art and recreation. Roughly speaking, we may say that industry consists in doing the necessary chores of life, while culture consists in carrying out the ultimate aims of life. Whatever these aims may be

—whatever is the greatest thing open to our earthly senses —one thing seems certain, namely, that ultimate human aspiration consists in one form or another of broadening our mental and spiritual horizon. Whatever is *limiting*, unless it be a base for something else, spells stagnation and death; whatever is *unlimiting* makes for eternal expansion and life. "An infinite expectation of the dawn." How may we "remodel" our environment to meet this expectation?

Environment, we have said, is "outward influence"—it is influx of energy. Niagara Falls possesses mechanical horse power—the influx of energy upon a whirling turbine; it possesses also psychologic horse power—the influx of energy upon the human soul. Each is a form of latent energy to be "developed" or converted to men's needs. Environment is developed through psychologic conversion. This consists in two forms of visualization: that of "stage" and that of "action." It is the action, the "act of living" itself, which concerns us now. An excellent statement of one aspect of the act of living, as here meant, is given by Mr. Aldo Leopold, of the United States Forest Service, in an article entitled "Wilderness as a Form of Land Use."[1] This particular statement relates to living in a particular environment, namely, the primeval environment, but it is suggestive of an approach to the larger problem of remodeling any setting through living in it. It is one of the very few contributions thus far to the psychology of regional planning. His set-up of the problem is, briefly, about as follows:

"The first idea is that wilderness is a resource . . . a distinctive environment which may, if rightly used, yield

[1] In the *Journal of Land and Public Utility Economics,* October, 1925.

certain social values." The wilderness is the environment of the American pioneers, something which "had values of its own and was not merely a punishment which they (the pioneers) endured in order that we might ride in motors." Pioneering is now ended in America; it is a "receding economic fact": but, like many another such, "it can be preserved for the ends of sport." The economic fact of *man vs. beast* has been preserved in the sport of hunting. The economic fact of *war* has been preserved (minus its "moral and physical retrogressions") in the sport of football. And so the economic fact of *pioneering* can be preserved in the sport and "act of living in the open." As the means for preserving the stage for such activity, Mr. Leopold visualizes the "wilderness area," embracing a sample of the primeval state in any or all degrees—"from the little accidental wild spot at the head of a ravine in a corn belt woodlot to vast expanses of virgin country." Every open way or "levee" described in the previous chapter would be such a "wilderness." Mr. Leopold seems here to see both stage and action. The "wilderness area" forms the stage. The "act of living in the open" forms the activity.

Such, in a word, is Mr. Leopold's thesis. To my own mind it is a potent one. But "sport" (Mr. Leopold's word) seems offhand too small to fit the bigness of his idea. The development of this primal act of "living in the open," epitomizing as it does the full activity of man, is surely more inclusive than any single activity of the sportsman. It appears as something greater than mere sport unless we use the word in extension of the ordinary use and say again with Thoreau—"let not to get a living be thy trade, but thy *sport*." The word *art*, it seems to me, is in closer harmony with Mr. Leopold's discerning program. This art (or "sport," or what you will) embraces the equivalent of all athletics and far more; it is contact not alone of man to man but of man to the whole of nature: camping is rude industry, and home-making; "hiking" is incipient exploration; the song around the camp fire is the seed of the folk-play and of human melody. "The Open" is epitomized life.

The development of such an art has long been under way, and splendid beginnings have been made, here in America, by certain outdoor groups. But compared with the evident possibilities, most of us seem to be mere infants in the exclamatory stage. We walk the trail and exclaim, "Oh, ain't it beautiful!"—and let it go at that. We do as Christien does in Rostand's play *Cyrano de Bergerac*. When Christien looks upon Roxanne he appreciates the make-up of her body and soul: he appreciates what a friend of mine has called "that most beautiful product of natural evolution—a young girl." He does nothing, however, to further that evolution in the realm of human mind. But Cyrano does. All Christien can do is to say, "I love you; I love you *so!*" But Cyrano tells *how* he loves her; he tells what Christien really means by "so." And in so doing he takes his part in what Mr. Leopold refers to as "self-directed evolution": he develops for all mankind, through his poetic art, a deeper, fuller understanding of that mysterious and all-pervading medium which Christien can only call by name.

This all-pervading thing—call it beauty, power, spirit, or what you please—appears to us in various ways: it may be focused sharply—as in the image of the young girl; or it may be unfocused and diffused—as in the sweeping landscape. This thing we all appreciate. But how? If we do as Christien, we see the vision but carry nothing of it to our fellow beings: we leave it in its latency. But if, in however slight degree, we do as Cyrano, then we ourselves take part in "focusing"; and, by making latent beauty visible, develop the realm of art. In order, therefore, to bring the latent energy of the primeval environment to the full of human benefit there is more to do than just to have a wilderness and walk aimlessly about it. We cannot all be Cyrano, but we can all aspire; and to the extent that we so do we become thereby "little Cyranos." By practicing strenuously the *act*, we can in time develop the full *art* of "living in the open."

The primeval environment we have placed as one of the so-called "elemental environments," the communal and the urban being the others. Together these form the indigenous environment—that which innately belongs to the soil and the human mind in contrast to the intrusive influence of the metropolis which does "not belong." The primeval environment, as already pointed out, is seen to form, on close analysis, the one environment which is truly elemental; for out of this come all the others. It is the mother of the indigenous environment: it forms the outward setting for the contact of man and nature, but in it lies the seed also of the relation—man and man. Let us set up the three elemental human contacts which go, roughly speaking, with the three elemental settings. They are:

The contact of man and nature—capable of permanent development in the primeval setting.

The all-round symmetric contact of man and man—capable presumably of highest development in the communal setting, the "neighborhood."

The specialized contact of man and man—which has developed for the most part in the urban setting, the city proper.

The communal setting grows out of the primeval, while the urban is a compound of the communal. The notion of the "regional city," whose specifications we have already crudely sketched, would combine all three of these. I have in mind, for illustration, a certain small city in New England whose tributary territory (that embraced within an hour's drive by motor) contains potentially the settings and contacts named. A small mountainous and pastoral area in the northwest corner provides the primeval (or near-primeval) contact; each one of some forty typical New England villages within the territory provides a base for developing the communal contact; the totality of such villages connected by a framework of intervillage highways would form a compound community providing for the urban (or group) contacts. This is not a "plan," it is a physical possibility; it might or might not be revealed as of innate consequence.

Each one of the three settings and contacts just named constitutes the subject for developing a definite portion of the art of "living in the open." Three distinct situations are provided for developing definite lines of activity. Each line of action would emanate naturally from a specific site.

One line of action would spread outward from the *camp fire*. Speaking geographically, the zone covered by this action would embrace what Mr. Leopold would call a "wilderness area" or open way. Through the instrumentality of cabin and trail, the wilderness area would be developed as a primeval (or near-primeval) environment. This line of work would (and does) constitute the primary step perhaps in developing the "act" or "sport" or "art" of living in the open. This particular field of endeavor is being developed, in the several regions of America, by various outing and outdoor groups like those represented in such gatherings as the New England Trail Conference.

Another line of action would radiate from the *village green*. The zone covered would embrace the village Common and community and the surrounding rural area which is naturally tributary thereto. This area would be developed as a communal environment. In the case of New England the innate setting would be revealed most likely as some form of the colonial mold. Dealing with the outward general life of the community, and not with the inner particular life of the individual, the activity involved would constitute an extension of the art of living in the open. Certain activities, literally speaking, must be carried on under roof: the home folks might gather in the town hall just as the campers would gather in the mountain cabin. This particular field of endeavor is now making its beginnings in various parts of America. I do not mean the dogmatic attempts, of long-time standing, toward village improvement and civic betterment; I refer to the keen attempts toward revealing and dramatizing the indigenous communal life made by such groups as the Little Country Theater of North Dakota and the Carolina Players.

A third line of action would emanate from the *wayside*. The zone here covered would consist of the abutting land and aspects along the inter-village highways; in other words, the intertown. This zone would be developed as a fitting and suitable link in the framework of the "regional city." This does not mean that it would be an urban environment; on the contrary it would be a rural environment. *By no means* would it be a suburban environment. The zone would be developed as far as possible as an attractive passageway between one village and another, and in this sense would become a part of the total environment of the regional city. The purpose of the work involved would be as far as possible to complete the setting for a life "in the open." The first steps in this endeavor are now being taken by those rising strenuous groups of general "appreciators" who are beginning to wage a dogged war on billboards, "hot-dog kennels," and the other metropolitan personifications of wayside desecration. I refer to protectors of the countryside such as are represented in the various local and State committees on the billboard nuisance; I refer also to those revealers of the latent countryside who by visualizing and establishing artistic settings for tea houses and other intertown utilities, in harmony with local surroundings and picturesque tradition, are developing, in positive manner, the potential resource of the wayside environment.

The job to do in each one of these developments is not to "plan" but to *reveal*—to seek the innate design of forces higher than our limited powers. We have taken a whole chapter to explain that planning is fundamentally revelation. Let us never forget this. The true planner is a seeker —a revealer: he must guard himself from dogma as he would from poison. This is a special admonition to the technical planner. And the best guard he can procure is the amateur planner. The point may be made that the technician unsupported by the people and a public consciousness is a head without a body, and that the public at large, unguided by technical advice, is a body without a head. The amateur in any line is a representative of the best thought of the public at large—he is the forerunner of the ultimate conviction of an advancing public opinion: for this reason he is the ally *par excellence* of the technician. Let the technical planner or "revealer" ally himself closely with a body of amateur revealers: then shall we have a body *with* a head. We have just been referring to certain types of amateur revealers—the camper, the player, the "general appreciator": let us make a closer canvas of these amateur assistants.

There is the amateur revealer of Mother Earth herself —of the earth's surface as carved and uplifted and carved again by the cosmic forces. This is the would-be geographer and geologist—the "Little Humboldt," if you please. There is the revealer of the earth's wild life, as it has evolved out of that "indefinite past" of which Lincoln spoke. This is the student of natural history—the botanist, the ornithologist, and the others—the little "Darwins" and "Audubons." The special province of these amateurs is the primeval environment; they stand high among the real users of the cabin and the trail: their field of activity and romance lies within sight of the camp fire.

There is the amateur revealer of the story of mankind— the past story and the future story. This is revealed to us in its human intimacy through the local history of a region's settlement, and in the general community life springing from such settlement. Here is the field of the local historian, the historical writer and dramatist, and the Egglestons and Hawthornes of the region. I refer not to mere delvers in the past. I refer to the seekers of that which "belongs to the ages" and not to any special generation. Eggleston has preserved for us a chapter of American life—that of the Hoosier town. Hawthorne has given us, in *The Scarlet Letter* and *The House of the Seven Gables,* a picture of colonial New England; and Owen Wister, in his *Virginian,* has captured the primitive western utopia of the cow-puncher. Through each of these and through every other indigenous American story (whether captured or yet at large) there runs a stream of permanent American purpose (and world-purpose). The historian or dramatist whom I have in mind is the one who, like the authors just named, would aspire to reveal that "stream" —he who would develop a portion, however tiny, of that stream's potential "horse power" toward the upbuilding of a future world. Let us, to get down to a prosaic and utilitarian example, reveal and restore the color and atmosphere of the old colonial mansion, built perhaps upon a cellar hole exuding tradition, and then, in our "plans," install a modern bathroom. Let us, in short, combine the virtues of the ancient and permanent with those of the modern and permanent. Thus may we keep abreast of the "stream" and develop its full "horse power."

Next there is the revealer of the community's play life. I refer especially to the folk-play—the song and dance and the various outdoor sports going with the season and the time of day. Here is another vital opportunity for the would-be dramatist, and particularly the musician-dramatist. Here is a field of permanent rhythm and melody awaiting the hand of the "little Wagner" or the coming of another Gilbert and Sullivan. Through the skillful tuning up of the strains latent in "Lady Walpole's Reel" and "Turkey in the Straw" there is opened a way toward a "listening in" on what seems to be a portion of that basic symphony itself lying at the bottom of indigenous life and comradeship. Here is an outlet for youthful sensibilities which, when shorn of ancient Puritan inhibition, is charged sufficiently with its own intrinsic joy and healthful abandon to elude safely the short-circuiting indulgences of a metropolitan—and courtezan—environment.

The field of activity and romance belonging to the two last-named "revealers"—to the embryonic Hawthornes and to the little Wagners—emanates from the village green. Its sphere of influence embraces the community as such, the "unit of humanity" with its starfish symmetry of structure and its latent symphonious human function of all-round social contact. Its special province is the communal environment.

There is no class of revealer that I know of whose special province is the urban environment. The life of the true city we have stated as being one of numerous specialties and groups. But there is a class of revealers whose province might be said to be the environment of the thing which we have described under the term of "regional city." These revealers consist of a class of what we have referred to as "general appreciators"—those persons who, motivated usually by an artistic sense, instinctively seek a symmetric and symphonious setting both for the community and for the national life. They rank high in numbers, but thus far have not been integrated in any common movement. They are found in the ranks of such movements as those for establishing national parks and forests, and for the eradication of city slums. They consist largely of fighters against specific evils, though for the most part they are not lacking in constructive sense. They are at bottom positive artists, not negative fighters. The particular value of such revealers with respect to our present problem would lie in their possible interest in the general framework of the regional city. This framework is in a sense the cement which binds the three elemental environments within a region. The heart of this framework lies in the inter-village highway, or "intertown." Here is an environment all its own—*the wayside environment.* The wayside is a cross-section of the countryside. And right here we have the special province of this class of would-be, or amateur, landscape-makers. Their special field of activity would come, not from the camp fire nor from the village green, but from the wayside.

There is one class of revealer whose field of activity emanates from all three environments—that of the camp fire, that of the village green, and that of the wayside. This is the artist proper—the landscape painter or even the amateur photographer. He brings the comprehensive notion to the eye as the musical artist brings it to the ear. Each of the revealers we have mentioned—naturalist, historian, dramatist, artist—is engaged in the imaging, on paper or canvas or other vicarious medium, of the vital forces, rhythms, and aspects of definite desirable environments. Could their efforts, properly mobilized and focused, achieve a revelation of these selfsame forces in a medium more vital and more real? This apparently was the query in the back of Thoreau's head when he pointed out the latent consummation which in these chapters has been emphasized. He says:

It is something to be able to paint a particular picture, or to carve a statue, and so to make a few objects beautiful; but it is far more glorious to carve and paint the very atmosphere and medium through which we look. . . . To affect the quality of the day, that is the highest of arts.

"The very atmosphere and medium through which we look." Here is the common mind which we have called *environment;* it is the "quality of the day": to "affect" it is the "highest of arts." Such is the consummation awaiting the combined vision and sensibility of the various classes of "revealers" we have mentioned. The art of the drama came about as a synthesis of the other arts. The "art" of developing environment, of "living in the open," of "affecting the quality of the day," seems by natural and inevitable steps to be forthcoming as another and greater synthesis.

Another name for art is culture. To this particular type of culture I have elsewhere adapted a term once used by Mr. Chauncey J. Hamlin of Buffalo, New York. His term is "Outdoor Culture." [2] Outdoor culture is the dramatization of the countryside. But it is not so much an affecting of the countryside as of *ourselves* who are to live in it. After all, it is ourselves and not the land, whose happiness is affected. The way to get more fun and zest out of playing and living within our native land and field is the same way as to get more fun out of playing on the football field: it is to know "the game" better—to know the *art* better. In developing ourselves in the man-to-man contact of football, we develop the whole environment of virile athletic sport; in developing ourselves in other tangible contacts— by the camp fire, in the village gathering, and along the wayside—we develop other tangible environments whose combined power constitutes "the day" itself. In this wise —in developing ourselves to demand the best in life—do

[2] Mr. Hamlin coined this term at a meeting in 1925, in Washington, of the President's Conference on Outdoor Recreation.

we build the kind of world that the human mind ultimately seeks.

Lewis Mumford, as already mentioned, has pointed out to us two distinct types of utopia: the utopia of escape and the utopia of reconstruction. Here is our choice: between the make-believe and the real. Shall we go to the play and for the time being become a big vicarious Cyrano and let it go at that?—or shall we, in addition, capture the spirit of our hero and resolve to become real, if diminutive, Cyranos? Our job in the new exploration is nothing short of making a utopia of reconstruction—the remodeling of an unshapen and cacophonous environment into a humanized and well-ordered one. This is something which the technical "planner" cannot do alone: he requires the close alliance of the amateur revealer of life's setting, and above all of human life itself. To remodel our house properly, we must live in it. To remodel "the open," we must learn the art of "living in the open." This art is in the making. It is the coming synthetic art—call it outdoor culture or what you will—which, from camp fire and village and wayside, is even now radiating its vital influence and beginning to find itself. And so we begin to realize Thoreau's dream and prophecy, and to take part each in our humble path in affecting the quality itself of our common mind and day.

Chapter XIV

CULTURE VS. MECHANIZATION

Over-civilized people are beginning to find out that going to the mountains is going home.—JOHN MUIR.

The mountains represent the thing which in the blunt terms of our technical jargon we have called the "primeval environment." And this is the seed of the whole indigenous environment: for the communal derives from the primeval and the urban from the communal. So the camp fire is our primal "home." But the metropolitan environment is no portion of our home. It is a thing exotic which does not "belong." It is a product of the "over-civilized." The indigenous is the atmosphere of the home ideal—of the innate, the permanent, and the complete: the metropolitan is the atmosphere of ideals astray—of the exotic, the temporary, the unbalanced, and the distorted. One is complete: the other is partial and makeshift.

There is tragic confusion on this point. This confusion is greatest in the city. Each city really is two cities—the metropolitan city and the indigenous or truly urban city. But the two are inordinately mixed. This confusion in the hazy landscape—in the outer world which is our common mind—makes a confusion in every one of us, each in his inner mind. It makes a haze within ourselves. And with *ourselves*—more than the landscape—must we ultimately deal. What is our outlook, our attitude, toward the outer world which we must share? Our outlook—toward *any-*

thing—comes from our inmost thoughts. Mencken says (concerning the metropolitan) that there is a "voluptuous quality" to it. Is *this* our attitude? Are we as a people mentally astray with regard to the landscape and outer human relations, as the roué is astray with regard to intimate human relations? Do we produce for ourselves, with one portion of our personality, that which our whole personality—if integrated—would certainly reject?

The distinction between urban and metropolitan (between indigenous, as a whole, and metropolitan) is nothing less, as I understand it, than the distinction made by Spengler between "culture" and "civilization." One is the tendency in society (and in ourselves) to develop and to *grow*, while the other is the tendency to become mechanized and then merely to *expand*. One is an evolution of mind, the other—a multiplication of facts: a Shakespeare is an outcome of the one, the bathroom is a product of the other. Both are useful and important: culture evolves the ends of life, civilization produces the means of life; one is living, the other is "getting ready to live." Civilization properly used results in culture: civilization worshiped for its own sake becomes over-civilization; its ultimate is an animated mechanization. This term "mechanization" states more explicitly perhaps what Spengler means by "civilization."

In an over-civilization both work and play are mechanized. The worker tends to become the "iron man"—the grim clanking automaton shown in Čapek's play *R.U.R.*, or the wound-up chirping clerk depicted by Elmer Rice in his *Adding Machine*. Here is a picture of *toil* carried to its logical conclusion. And a picture might be made of another logical conclusion. As toil is the degenerate element of work, so *decreation* is a name for the degenerate element of play. Čapek, or somebody else, should write a play depicting decreation carried to conclusion. This play might focus on some tea table about 5 P.M. in some ornate tomb on the twenty-ninth floor of the latest apartment house where innately good if over-polished people gather to discourse assiduously on the relative merits of their bathroom sets, their window curtains, their motor oils, and their other intricate means, within the sign-decked and encumbered limits of their horizon, for dressing up and going nowhere. The scene could be laid in New York or in Singapore: it would make no difference—the apartment house would be the same, and the tea-tomb, and all the other properties—as well as the conversation thereabout. No, it would not be conversation, it would be what Owen Wister calls "routine." Real conversation widens the horizon, while routine (out of its proper place—in business) merely encumbers the horizon. One goes with mental enlightenment and recreation; the other goes with mental obtusion and decreation: one is the language of the cultured, the other of the over-civilized. In an over-civilization both work and play are mechanized.

"Culture," then, we might say, consists of the development or continuous regeneration of work and play—into *art* on the one side and *recreation* on the other. "Civilization" (not used as a means, but worshiped as an end) consists of the degeneration of work and play—into *toil* on the one side and *decreation* on the other.

Spengler speaks of "Greek culture" and "Roman civilization." In all human relations—whether outward or intimate—there seem to be these two attitudes: the Greek and the Roman. Lest some historian should pick me up as an amateur upon this point let me revise this statement: there are two attitudes toward life—the one aroused by the *myth* of "the Greek" and the one aroused by the *myth* of "the Roman." We have dwelt long in this book upon this mental cleavage. It is vital in the New Exploration. This cleavage represents the great conflict lying in the background of our present-day problems of planning and revelation. It is the *issue* of regional planning considered as a social movement. Indigenous versus metropolitan; culture versus mechanization.

We have attempted in the preceding chapters to present various phases of this issue. The indigenous and the metropolitan we first visualized from the top of Mt. Monadnock; we traced briefly the spread of the latter over the former both in America and throughout the world; we analyzed the nature of each environment—one suited to *living* and the other to *existence* merely; we have suggested ways and means for controlling the one environment and developing the other. Let us now in these concluding paragraphs attempt to visualize the issue as a whole. In this we shall use the rough but telling method of analogy, for it is necessary to epitomize in a single glance the movements of all of Western history as these affect our issue. I shall borrow Herr Spengler's graphic idea of the cycle of society and its four seasons, and shall, as an amateur, present, briefly and crudely, my own myth and visualization.

The history of Western nations emerges vaguely during the early centuries of the Mediterranean Epoch. The first heroes of this drama are a crowd of frontiersmen or barbarians. They are the Homeric Greeks. The first of their famed exploits that we read about is their destruction of the Cretan city of Cnossus. This is the swift punishment placed upon the Cretans for attempting to practice on the Greeks what we today would call the "white slave trade." This good old two-fisted story of frontier justice comes down to us, in colorful guise, in the myth of Theseus and the Minotaur. But the first big authentic act of the drama is the resisting, and the vanquishing, by these frontiersmen, of what must have seemed at the time an overwhelming invasion. This is the Oriental invasion. It is focused in the Medes and Persians under the irresistible Darius. But he is met by Miltiades one September afternoon on the Plains of Marathon.

Until this September afternoon (490 years before Bethlehem) the Persians represent "civilization": Darius is a Civilized-one who sees Miltiades as a mere Barbarian. Says Creasy:

Before Marathon was fought, the prestige of success and of supposed superiority of race was on the side of the Asiatic against the European. Asia was the original seat of human societies, and long before any trace can be found of the inhabitants of the rest of the world having emerged from the rudest barbarism, we can perceive that mighty and brilliant empires flourished in the Asiatic continent. They appear before us through the twilight of primeval history, dim and indistinct, but massive and majestic, like mountains in the early dawn.

We shall not explore these "mountains" nor attempt to trace within them any cycles of society. We are exploring only in the Western world. Marathon marks the repulse of accepted (stabilized) "civilization": and it marks the rise of something else. It is a meeting and a struggle between two spirits: something deeper than West versus East—it is "infinite variety and restless change" versus "monotonous uniformity." Marathon, considered not as a battle of four hours' duration but as a recurrent event of eternal duration, is the meeting of the renascent versus the outworn—of the apt subtlety of youth versus the inert power of momentum; of the pliable force of growth versus the rigid power of expansion: the triumph of Marathon is one with that of the forest over the glacier and of the May flower over the snow bank. Marathon marks the coming of the "springtime" in a Mediterranean cycle of society— the harbinger of a *growing Greek culture* and the turning back of an *expanding Persian civilization*.

Marathon creates the opportunity for Pericles and Plato: a mechanization is dyked and a culture is allowed to flower—and the full summer of Greek glory comes to pass. Then (about three centuries B.C.) the storms of "autumn" appear—all too promptly. They come in person, as it were—the Roman and the Carthaginian. These persons are neither frontiersmen nor barbarians. Quite the contrary: they have dwelt upon the Mediterranean as long as have the Greeks, on whose arts of war and peace they have long been scavenging. They have frozen the Greek culture into a glacier of civilization, and their ambition now is to expand that glacier. But which one will expand it—the Roman or the Carthaginian? They take a century to decide this little matter—in the Punic Wars, the most desolate struggle perhaps in all the long tragedy of warfare. The Roman beats. This creates the opportunity for Julius Caesar and the full winter of Roman would-be glory —the glory of expansion versus that of growth. For Rome

has now captured "the world" and rules the Mediterranean.

The Roman type needs no emphasis. It is emphasis itself. It is the apotheosis of the thing which John Muir
might call the "over-civilized," or what the Brook Farm
people would have called the "Civilizee." If you want to
know what I mean go to the photo-play *Ben-Hur* and look
upon Messala, the helmeted Roman officer.

Well, this is the gentleman who runs the Mediterranean
world in the dawn of the Christian era. He continues to run
it for about five centuries. But his foot is always slipping.
His glacier of civilization is shrinking and breaking up.
Out east in Asia Minor and Egypt and Greece it splits into
separate fragments under the guise of an Eastern Roman-
ism. And then one day appears, out of the north and out
of "the world," once more the Barbarian. One of his
names is "Goth." He takes charge in Italy of such fragments as remain of the strenuous winter orgies; and Rome,
as Rome, falls forever out of the world's geography.

But the Goth is not to the Roman what the Greek once
was to the Persian. He marks the end of winter, but not
the real beginning of spring. He is, however, the promise of
spring—like the ground hog in February. But the spring
this time is late—very late—about six hundred years late.
For winter takes a long relapse—known as the Dark Ages.
The Christian Church takes charge of the world, as the
Roman power did before: it tells the people what to think.
And they obey—all but a few. These few think for themselves; in the fifteenth century these intellectual adven-
turers begin to increase. They break away from the rigid
abstractions of "eternity" which the Church feeds out
to them. What about *this* world anyhow? Is the Mediter-

ranean the whole of it? How about the East? Ah, the East! The land found by Marco Polo—land of spices, of elephants—of India! The lure of something "out there" —not in heaven, but here on earth! Let us go.

And so history becomes a "sudden stream of purpose"—the Reformation and the Renaissance; the men of science—da Vinci, Copernicus, and Galileo; the explorers —da Gama, Columbus, and Magellan. Spiritually and cosmically this "stream" is searching the *terra incognita* of the universe; geographically it is headed for the East. The Church and its dogmas attempt to block one stream, while the Turks attempt to block the other. This makes the pressures all the harder. For spiritual reasons as well as worldly, the people want to break away. The Turks capture Constantinople in 1453. All the careful plans for going Eastward overland are broken up (plans for "A, B, C, and D" must be put aside, for "E" has happened). So Columbus appears with "Plan E"—to go east he will sail *west!* He starts. Magellan follows, and his little ship, the *Victoria,* is the first to sail around the globe. And so through these frontiersmen of the sea the Epoch of the Oceans is unfolded. It is a time when new ideas are growing—not old ones just expanding.

There follows a short summer season. Shakespeare comes and the Elizabethan period of arts and letters. The eternal melodies are heard again, something as they were in Grecian times. And the eternal mysteries are visioned as they never were before: the glimpses obtained by Eratosthenes and Aristotle are developed and revealed by Copernicus and Newton and Faraday and Humboldt and Darwin, and we find where we are among the stars, and within the great course of evolution. Strenuous centuries these—

from the sixteenth to the nineteenth! Perhaps too strenuous. For science takes to the "material fact" to the
neglect of the "spiritual form." Matter is a readier medium
than spirit for the matter-of-fact processes of science and
so the machinery of life takes on a bound. Between Watt
and Stephenson and others the steam engine is born, and
this in turn gives birth to the modern factory, the steamship, and the "iron horse." The magician of harnessed
electricity then shows up, and motor transportation; intricate processes of metallurgy are developed—and the
iron age, through this the *industrial revolution,* comes for
the first time into full blast.

Alas! . . . An over-fruitful summer brings a hastened
autumn. While Darwin is still working, the glacier of iron
industrialism (of iron civilization and mechanization)
begins its grim expansion. And the storms of autumn begin
again—even as in the days of Rome and Carthage. They
begin before the iron horse is born—or the iron steamship:
they begin right after Columbus and Magellan—while
Copernicus is still at work. The stage is being set for the
spread of the iron glacier itself when in the twentieth century it starts on its modern journey. Pope Alexander VI in
1494 divides the outside world between Spain and Portu-
gal. This makes Spain and England rivals. Sir Francis
Drake destroys the Spanish Armada in 1588. Then it is
England versus France, and the potential empire of America is taken by the British General Wolfe out of the hands
of the French General Montcalm at Quebec in 1759. The
British conquest of India takes place in the same decade.
And later on, in 1914, with the race eastward of the Ger-
man iron horse going via Bagdad against the British
steamship going through Suez, the mastery of world-ex-

pansion is fought out once more. Britain, nominally at
least, captures the directorship of the "iron glacier" in
this its modern journey. But America, an iron empire in
itself, with frontage on two oceans connected by Panama,
is a potentiality greater than all Britain. Whether the
modern Rome and Carthage will fight it out once more;
or whether, combining, they will direct between them the
spread and flow of iron industrialism and metropolitanism
—one thing seems evident: that the flow itself is under
way throughout the world. Indigenous India, indigenous
China, and (what concerns us most) *indigenous America,*
are under invasion by the iron glacier: it is spreading, as
a "metropolitan flow," out along the highways from each
metropolis, large and small—out of New York and out
of "Zenith." Indigenous innate "culture" is overtaken by
metropolitan intrusive "civilization" (and mechanization).
Spengler's "winter" is come again.

If winter comes, can spring be far behind?
That is the question. Will the coming spring be late or
early? Are we in for another Roman régime or another
Middle Ages? *Or* may the industrial revolution (potent in
precipitating an autumn and a winter) be made, through
a vision of its workings, to direct its titanic powers to a
prompt achievement of true freedom, and thus to the coming of an equable cultural climate, like that of the Mediterranean zone, without extremes of cold or heat? Can
centuries be speeded into decades? "Impossible," we say;
and yet we do not know. Let us not be caught by Spengler's dark metaphor. For we have reached a new frontier
in the journey of history. Pygmies have become centaurs.
The weakling man, seated in his motor car with hand on

wheel and foot on lever, becomes a locomotive running forty miles an hour. Here is distance—how about direction? Can he, through sufficient understanding of his acquired powers, guide a triumphant means toward achieving some real and ultimate end and not merely in attaining further *means?*

But whether spring be late or early, we find ourselves in the shoes of our forefathers. They were confronted by a wilderness of nature; we are invested by a wilderness of civilization. This is a wilderness of near-infinite complexity; it is one also of monotonous, standardized, mechanized uniformity. And, what is of chief significance, it is a wilderness which *"flows."* We are invested not merely by a wilderness of civilization, but by an invasion of civilization. We have called it the metropolitan invasion. This must be met—and dyked. Here is something which cannot all at once be done in some spectacular fashion on a September afternoon—as the Persian invasion was met on the plains of Marathon: instead it must be dyked in small sectors, one at a time, by some system of embankments—or "levees"; and this with all the ingenuity and patience required in dyking and controlling the invasion and floodings of a Mississippi River.

These dykes and levees consist, broadly viewed, of what John Muir calls "the mountains"—of the primeval areas, and the seats of our primal home. These form the indigenous base for controlling the metropolitan invasion and the spread of its mechanized metropolitan environment. And they form the base for developing the indigenous environment. In this our innate "basic America" (and basic world generally), there has recently been working—indeed since Thoreau's time—what we have called a synthesis of arts whose goal we have said is nothing less than "to affect the quality of the day." And through such base and leverage, fully utilized, should our faith be keen in our ability to hold in check the flow and expansion of a one-sided *civilization,* and advance the growth of an all-sided *culture.*

The two types of wilderness of which we have just spoken (nature's wilderness and civilization's) form the subject of the two types of exploration which we recounted in the first portion of this book—the old exploration and the new. Each is a dispelling of confusion. Each perhaps has its occasion to bring it to fulfillment. The fall of Constantinople in 1453 (coming overnight) was the *occasion* for the world's great navigations and discoveries—the dispelling of the confusion of the labyrinth of continents. The coming of the industrial revolution (within a century), precipitating as it has the metropolitan flood (within a generation), marks another "overnight event" in history's perspective. May this be perhaps the *occasion* for dispelling another confusion—that of the labyrinth of civilization?

The forces set loose in the jungle of our present civilization may prove more fierce than any beasts found in the jungle of the continents—far more terrible than any storms encountered within uncharted seas. Here in America—particularly in Appalachian America—we have an area which, potentially, is perhaps the most "volcanic" of any area on earth. It is an area laden with the ingredients of modern industry and civilization: iron, coal, timber, petroleum. It is electric with a high potential—for human happiness or human misery. The coal and iron pockets which lie beneath the surface may be the seeds of freedom or seeds of bitterness; for in them is the latent substance of distant foreign wars as well as deep domestic strife.

These forces are neither "good" nor "bad" but *so.* And they do not stand still, but flow and spread as we have told. Can we control their flow before it controls us? Can we do it *soon enough?* This is a crucial question of our day. What instructions can we issue to our modern-day explorer (whether technician or amateur) to guide him in coping with this modern-day invasion?

The new explorer, of this "volcanic" country of America, must first of all be fit for all-round action: he must combine the engineer, the artist, and the military general. It is not for him to "make the country," but it is for him to know the country and the trenchant flows that are taking place upon it. He must not scheme, he must reveal: he must reveal so well the possibilities of A, B, C, and D that when E happens he can handle it. His job is not to wage war—nor stress an argument: it is to "wage" a determined *visualization.* His attitude in this must be one not of frozen dogma or irritated tension, but of gentle and reposeful power: he must speak softly but carry a big map. He need not be a crank, he may not be a hero, but he must be a scout. His place is on the frontier—within life's "cambium layer"—the fluid twilight zone of all creative action in which the flickering thoughts of future are woven in the structure of the past. . . . And our last instruction to our new explorer and frontiersman is to hold ever in sight his final goal—to reveal within our innate country, despite the fogs and chaos of cacophonous mechanization, *a land in which to live*—a symphonious environment of melody and mystery in which, throughout all ages, we shall "learn to reawaken and keep ourselves awake, not by mechanical aids," but by that "infinite expectation of the dawn" which faces the horizon of an ever-widening vision.

Appendix

THE TOWNLESS HIGHWAY

The design of automobiles took years to outgrow the fallacious notion that the motor car was just a horseless buggy. Our motor highways are still in much the same predicament that automobile design was in thirty years ago. Even our most modern roads, modern in the sense that they have solid foundations and concrete surfaces and banks at the sharp turns, are conceived as mere extensions and widenings of the old-fashioned highway design for horse-drawn vehicles.

Actually, the motor road is a new kind of road, as different from the old-fashioned highway as the railroad was; and it demands, accordingly, a new type of plan. The logical development of the modern motor road, from the standpoint of transporting people and goods and guiding the new migration of population, is in the direction of the townless highway. In contrast with the Utopia of Roadtown, which Mr. Edgar Chambless published a few decades ago, the modern regional planner arrives at just the opposite solution: namely, a highway completely free of horses, carriages, pedestrians, towns, grade crossings; a highway built for the motorist and kept free from every encroachment, except the filling stations and restaurants necessary for his convenience. Motor traffic and pedestrian "living" do not go together. To insulate each activity is a prime condition for speed and convenience on the one hand, and for safety and peace of mind, to say nothing of freedom from noise and carbon monoxide, on the other.

We shall see how necessary and inevitable the townless highway is if we recall the main characteristics of our earlier periods of transportation.

(Reprinted from *The New Republic* of March 12, 1930)

The first migration of the American people was led by the covered wagon; the next migration was led by the iron horse, which located the railroad framework of the country and gave importance and prestige to the terminal and junction towns. The present migration of population is being conducted by the automobile; and while a *future* one may result from the airplane, there is no reason to think that surface transportation will disappear in any *early* future, although the two may become more closely coördinated. Accordingly, it is with the present migration that we must intelligently deal. Today's migration consists of a drift, more or less automatic and unplanned, from the principal cities, out along the main highways. The modern motor road has accordingly two distinct functions: one is transportation, or the immediate flow of people and goods, and the other is migration, or the relocation of the population on the map of the United States. Both the ox-team trail and the railway had this dual role. The earliest type of transportation furthered the multiplication of villages and small country towns, in relation to the agricultural hinterland; the railway, throughout large portions of the country, definitely located most of the major industrial towns; and now today the motorway is blindly creating still another set-up.

As guided by the ox-team and the railway, the American migration westward represented a crude and pioneer civilization; it lacked in large degree the physical conveniences and refinements of modern existence — the bathroom, the electric light, the telephone and private motor transport. But with all its shortcomings, this earlier civilization possessed, through the sheer accident of nature and geographic distribution, the physical basis for a genuine culture which might hold its own with any of its European origins: it possessed an unspoiled natural background and a choice of environments in which to live. Before 1900, an American could live in the city, or in the country, or in the backwoods. He had a choice of contacts — the great world of metropolitan affiliations and interests, or the great spirit of the wilderness untouched by man, or the contact of friend and neighbor in the smaller home community. In short, the nineteenth-century American, though ideologically a complete individualist, had, as a fact of daily experience, the environment of community; he had also the environment of the open spaces — the forest on the mountain, the field by the wayside, or easy access to the open sea. All these primary types of environments are now in danger of extinction; the community and the open wayside are both on the point of being overwhelmed and obliterated by the present-day uncontrolled migration led by the motor car.

The motor car is a deceptive creature. As a result of its origin, we still think of it as a homely and companionable vehicle, like the old buggy, when in hard fact it is a species as distinct as the locomotive. By a similar transfer of habit, we have until very recently looked upon the motor road as a fitting frontage for our home lot, instead of regarding it realistically as a causeway, as much to be shunned as a railroad. Once these conventional prejudices are abolished, we see that the motor road is a new kind of railroad; although it has many features that make it quite distinct from that type of transportation. For one thing, this new "locomotive" swings into the track at any point along the line; for another, it runs both ways on a one-track road, and safety is based on the technique of remaining stolidly in line or becoming an artful dodger. Since the gasoline locomotive can enter at any point, it follows that continuous rows of buildings can flank the highway on either side; and thus arises that continuous haphazard wayside development known as the "motor slum." As the outcome of this purely automatic and unintelligent adaptation to a new means of transport, we have today an unsafe means of transportation and an uncivic channel of migration. The motor slum in the open country is today as massive a piece of defilement as the worst of the old-fashioned urban industrial slums; and highway transportation that leads through the hearts of our cities and villages, making every crossing a grade crossing, is safe for neither motorist nor pedestrian.

The cure for this double failure and this growing evil is to take more seriously our new means of transportation, and to create for it new communal forms that correspond with its new functions. We must provide for properly guarded approaches to, and crossings of, the main motor highways at proper intervals; we must provide stopping places or stations, from each of which a side road will lead to the adjacent town with its business quarters and its properly secluded residential sections; we must take possession of the surrounding right-of-way, keeping it free from haphazard commercial development and obtaining for the benefit of the motorist the pleasant views and aspects of the country, unsullied by the rowdy clamor of billboard advertising. This may seem a large program; but actually it is merely the safe minimum demanded; and when one considers the loss to life and property and health and pleasure occasioned by our present methods of motor-road building, the price is but a small one to pay.

One bold start has already been made in the direction of adapting the motor car to an effective community life; and that is in the little city of Radburn, New Jersey, now being built by the City Housing Corporation of New York. This is the first attempt to think through the implications of modern transportation, and the demonstration that has been made here is not merely of prime importance to city planners: it is in truth a pattern for modern highway development beyond the limits of the city. Radburn consists, with respect to its road system, of a skeleton of major avenues and highways connected with the actual residential streets, which are a series of related cul-de-sacs backed by open park land. The home never comes in direct contact with the main motorway: the dwelling house fronts on a lane by which the motor car can enter and depart, but which it can never pass through. The pedestrian has his own footways, which are divorced from the motorways; the footway crosses the motorway by an underpass: in short, the grade crossing has been abolished. This means that through traffic can proceed along the major avenues without hindrance; it also means that the motor car entering the residential cul-de-sac is unhurried by the push of traffic from behind. In Radburn, in other words, the town is located "off the railroad" and the "railroad" is unimpeded by the town: each one gets rid of the other and profits by the isolation.

This happy divorce has sometimes been achieved by natural accident when by the grace of topography a thoroughfare runs through a valley and leaves an old village on top of a hill. The townless highway would repeat this practice, by design and not by accident. The townless highway is a motorway, in which the adjoining towns would be in the same relationship to the road as the residential cul-de-sacs in Radburn are to the main traffic avenues. What Radburn does in the local community, the townless highway would do for the country at large. This is genuine motor-way planning — as opposed to the backward and conventional planning in which we now sink millions of dollars of the community's money. Instead of a single roadtown slum, congealing between our big cities, the townless highway would encourage the building of real communities at definite and favorable points *off* the main road. The cul-de-sac town is the necessary corollary of safe and swift major transportation arteries. Regional planning with these ends in view will in turn save both the local community and the open wayside environment, and give proper access to the wild places, instead of insidiously wiping out all these precious assets together.

The main aims and methods of the townless highway may now be summarized. There are four specific objectives:

(1) To abolish the motor slum, or roadtown, and develop the rural wayside environment. To attain this, certain measures are suggested: namely, the abolition of approaches to the main high-way except at certain points; public ownership, or effective public control through rigorous zoning, of the foreground along the right-of-way, the land to be purchased in advance of road construction, or to be obtained through excess condemnation; proper landscape development of the foreground, including the culture of shade trees and the strict regulation of telephone and electric-light lines; and finally, strict control of highway service-station development, including location, architecture, management of filling stations, eating places and other wayside utilities.

(2) To stimulate the growth of the distinct community, compactly planned and limited in size, like the old New England village or the modern Radburn. This involves avoidance by the highway of the small town or village and its approach via a side lane, or more than one. It also involves provision of side-lane approaches leading to prospective villages or communities, each such community to be laid out in accordance with approved modern town-planning principles, for economy, amenity, and preservation as a distinct community.

(3) To relieve both the through road and the local town from

unnecessary congestion and other sources of friction. To attain this, the highway should avoid each larger town and city by means of a by-pass around it.

(4) To insure safety alike to the through motorist and to the local population. This entails four measures: the abolition of grade crossings on both the railroad and the motor road; the use of safety traps at all approaches to the highway; the limitation of the use of the highway to a single purpose — passenger traffic, and the building of suitable express highways for motor-freight traffic; and finally, the double-tracking of the highway so as to make two separate parallel one-way roads at varying distances apart — the foreground on each road, including wherever practicable all land between the roads, to be in public ownership or control as already suggested.

A national highway policy based on these features would have a leverage at hand, namely, the fund in the United States Treasury now being annually appropriated for the federal-aided state roads. These appropriations could be made on the contingency that certain conditions (embodying specified features) be carried out. Such a policy could apply to new lines of road to be constructed and in part to present lines to be remodeled. The matter could be placed in the hands of some comprehensive body, such as the recently established Federal Traffic Commission or some other comprehensive board to be created for the purpose. It would, of course, require action by Congress.

Any highway policy should form part of a larger policy of national transportation and migration whose ultimate purpose would involve the relocation and redistribution of the American people. This larger policy would involve transportation "of," "by" and "for": transportation *of* passengers, of freight and parcels, of power, of light, of messages; transportation *by* land, by water, by air; transportation *for* industrial purposes, for recreational purposes, for general living. It would involve transmission line, telephone and radio as well as steamship and airplane, freight car and motor truck. It would require a broad-gauged regional and inter-regional planning such as that proposed recently by Mr. Thomas H. MacDonald, Chief of the United States Bureau of Public Roads, and by other far-seeing public men. Some central body, in close touch with the President and Congress on the one side and with the several states on the other, should have this task in hand. And a critical part of their super-plans, in the present phase of our history and resettlement, would seem to be a national system of federal-aided passenger motor roads to take the lead in guiding our people, in accordance with some definite policy, into appropriate communities and settings for furthering the cultural growth, and not merely the industrial expansion, of American civilization.

BENTON MACKAYE

Index

DATE DUE

OCT 1 6,76			
NOV 01 76			
GAYLORD			PRINTED IN U.S.A.